RUNNING
Outside
The
Comfort
Zone

RUNNING
Outside The Comfort Zone

AN EXPLORER'S GUIDE
TO THE EDGES *of* RUNNING

SUSAN LACKE

Boulder, Colorado

3002 Sterling Circle, Suite 100
Boulder, CO 80301–2338 USA

VeloPress is the leading publisher of books on endurance sports and is a division of Pocket Outdoor Media. Focused on cycling, triathlon, running, swimming, and nutrition/diet, VeloPress books help athletes achieve their goals of going faster and farther. Preview books and contact us at velopress.com.

Distributed in the United States and Canada by Ingram Publisher Services

Library of Congress Cataloging-in-Publication Data
Names: Lacke, Susan, author.
Title: Running outside the comfort zone : an explorer's guide to the edges of
    running / Susan Lacke.
Description: Boulder, CO, USA : VeloPress, [2019] |
Identifiers: LCCN 2018052923 (print) | LCCN 2018057643 (ebook) | ISBN
    9781948006002 (ebook) | ISBN 9781937715847 (pbk.)
Subjects: LCSH: Lacke, Susan. | Women runners--United States--Biography. |
    Running--Anecdotes. | Running races--Anecdotes.
Classification: LCC GV1061.15.L33 (ebook) | LCC GV1061.15.L33 A3 2019 (print)
    | DDC 796.42092--dc23
LC record available at https://lccn.loc.gov/2018052923

This paper meets the requirements of ANSI/NISO Z39.48-1992
(Permanence of Paper).

Art direction: Vicki Hopewell

Cover design: Megan Roy

Cover photograph: Amos Morgan

Other photography: Aliza Rae Photography, p. 243; Caliente Bare Dare 5K, p. 145; Comrades Marathon Association, p. 213; Dan Campbell, p. 21; iStock, pp. 15 and 81; Jubilee Paige, p. 49; Rick T. Wilking/Getty Images, p. 91; Salt Lake City Marathon, p. 123; all other images courtesy of Susan Lacke

19   20   21 / 10   9   8   7   6   5   4   3   2   1

To Carlos, who got me started
And to Neil, who makes every finish line worth crossing

CONTENTS

A YEAR OUTSIDE MY COMFORT ZONE

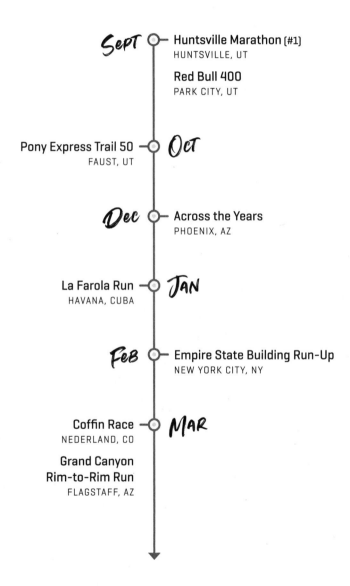

SepT

Huntsville Marathon [#1]
HUNTSVILLE, UT

Red Bull 400
PARK CITY, UT

Pony Express Trail 50
FAUST, UT

OcT

Dec

Across the Years
PHOENIX, AZ

La Farola Run
HAVANA, CUBA

JaN

FeB

Empire State Building Run-Up
NEW YORK CITY, NY

Coffin Race
NEDERLAND, CO

MaR

**Grand Canyon
Rim-to-Rim Run**
FLAGSTAFF, AZ

APR — Salt Lake City Marathon
SALT LAKE CITY, UT

Grand Blue Mile
DES MOINES, IA

Caliente Bare Dare 5K — **MAY**
LAND O' LAKES, FL

USA Network's
Storytellers Project
PHOENIX, AZ

Bay to Breakers
SAN FRANCISCO, CA

Cooper's Hill Cheese Roll
GLOUCESTER, ENGLAND

JUN — Girls on the Run Camp
SALT LAKE CITY, UT

Midwest Wife Carrying
Championship
FREDERICK, SD

Comrades Marathon
DURBAN, SOUTH AFRICA

Huntsville Marathon [#2] — **SEPT**
HUNTSVILLE, UT

INTRODUCTION

WHAT'S
THE PASSWORD?

I HAVE THE GREATEST JOB IN THE WORLD. As a writer of endurance sports, I get paid to chase endorphins on a daily basis. For almost a decade, I've written about the awe-inspiring feats of endurance athletes, from superhuman professionals covering an immense amount of terrain in a short time to everyday athletes who, against all odds, do the incredible. I've written hundreds of articles on endurance sports, interviewed some of the brightest minds in the biz, and participated in dozens of iconic triathlons and marathons around the world.

You'd think by now I'd have learned a thing or two about being an endurance athlete. Yet, if you're reading this book to learn the secret password for joining the runners' club, let me make one thing clear: You're reading the wrong book.

A few years ago, I was given the opportunity to write a different book—one that describes my journey from overweight, alcoholic chain-smoker to runner, triathlete, and fitness journalist. I didn't think anyone would care, honestly—after all, my story is the story of a lot of other endurance athletes out there. We're not born running up mountains. Most of us don't even figure out we're capable of such a feat until later in life. Along the way, we make a lot of mistakes. Some of us even hit rock bottom. And then we pick ourselves up, dust off the dirt, and start climbing—sometimes literally. Running is a transformative experience in mind, body, and spirit for so many. It helps us face inner demons and shush the naysayers—especially when those naysayers are ourselves.

So, I wrote about my climb, and something surprising happened when the book came out. People cared. In fact, they really liked the book! But when they approached me to tell me they liked it, I'd see their faces transform from excitement to bewilderment: "Oh, wow," they'd say. "I didn't know you were . . ."

And then they'd catch themselves before they said something truly offensive.

Let me back up a little bit. Despite being an endurance athlete, just plugging along, trying to climb the mountain as best as I can, I'm not your typical endurance athlete. I don't fit the mold for what most people expect from someone who writes about running for a living. Don't get me wrong—I love every square inch of my body. But I also love baked goods, and it shows. No matter how much I run, six-pack abs elude me, and my thighs are so curvaceous, so very sexy, they can't stop touching each other. I'm also not very fast. I've written articles about how to get faster, and yet my personal records, or PRs, are unimpressive. At best, I'm a middle-of-the-pack runner. Most days, I'm somewhere in the back. My written work is a classic case of "Do as I say, not as I do." After my first book came out, I'd get invited to group runs, only to sheepishly admit that . . . well, I wouldn't be able to maintain the average pace of that group. It was kind of embarrassing. I'm asthmatic, so every time I run, no matter how much fitness I have or what speed I'm going, I cough and wheeze like it's the first time I've gotten off the couch.

But the thing that really trips people up is my hearing aid. For years, I've written a lot about running and very little about the fact that I'm deaf. I have been since I was two and a half years old, when a virus killed off the nerve endings in my ears, rendering me completely deaf in one ear and what doctors call "severe-to-profoundly deaf" in the other. I wear one hearing aid in my so-called good ear, but it doesn't do much in the way of amplification—with it, I catch about 50 percent of what a hearing person can.

It wasn't a conscious decision to hide my disability in my writing. Honestly, it's all but impossible to hide. When you meet me, right from the second I say, "Hello," it's the most obvious thing about me. I rely on lipreading and will jockey for an ideal position to see your face. I speak the way I hear, which is to say, not very well. Every new conversation partner cocks his or her head like a springer spaniel, trying to place the foreign country behind my heavy accent.

When people can't remember my name, they refer to me as "the deaf one." It's never "the writer," "the runner," or even "the one with the brown hair." I would kill to be "the one with the brown hair." But no, it's "the deaf one." That is the quickest point of reference.

It's better than other names I've been called. When I was eight years old, my older brother, Chris, told me the kids in the neighborhood were building a fort. We excitedly rushed down to the end of the block, where we saw an elaborate structure constructed from tree branches and colorful bed sheets. A sign at the entrance declared, in crayon, **NO GROWN-UPS ALLOWED.** Chris and I stood there slack-jawed at just how cool it all was.

"Let's go in!" he said, running toward the entrance. I quickly followed. We were stopped by Elise, the oldest kid on the block.

"What's the password?" she said in a stern voice, her arms crossed across her chest. Chris and I looked at each other.

"Password?" I asked.

Elise nodded. "We need to make sure no grown-ups get in." To a group of kids, this logic made perfect sense.

"Open sesame?" Chris shrugged. Elise shook her head.

"Abracadabra?" Still no.

"Shazam?"

Elise rolled her eyes. "Fine, I'll tell you," she said, exasperated. She leaned in and whispered the password into his ear. Chris repeated it and was granted entry. The look on his face as he pulled back the curtain let me know something amazing was in store. I couldn't wait to get in.

"Come here," Elise said to me, leaning in. I pulled back, craning my neck to look at her mouth.

"I said," she sighed, "come *here.*"

"You can't whisper to her," Chris said. "She needs to see your mouth."

"But what if the grown-ups hear?" was her reply. We looked around—there wasn't a grown-up in sight. Still, if there was one thing we knew, it was that adults—moms, in particular—had supersonic hearing. We really couldn't be too careful.

"I got it," Chris said. Silently, he mouthed to me: "*The password is . . .*"

"The password is . . ." I parroted.

"*Super . . .*"

"Super!" I exclaimed. Elise shushed me—I was too loud. What if the grown-ups heard?

"What's the rest of it?" she demanded. I looked at my brother.

"*Cali . . .*"

"Colli?" It made no sense.

"*Fragi . . .*"

"What?" I squinted.

"*Fragi,*" he repeated, with urgency. He knew what was happening. I hadn't yet seen the movie *Mary Poppins*, and "super-califragilisticexpialidocious" was not in my vocabulary. *Super* was a word I recognized and could lip-read. The rest of it was gibberish, and I was racking my brain, trying to connect what my brother was saying to a word or phrase I recognized.

It was futile. As Chris repeated the word over and over, the kids from inside the fort stepped outside to see what was happening. With every failed attempt, I felt my face getting redder. And then it happened. I knew the words all too well.

"Your sister's retarded," Elise said.

The other kids thought it was funny. "Retard!" they laughed, slapping limp hands against their chests, mocking me. Hot tears stung my eyes. My brother sprinted out of the tent and grabbed my hand.

"Let's go."

"But the fort!" I cried.

"The fort's stupid," my brother huffed, yanking my arm. "Let's go."

My mom tried to console me that night, telling me it would get better. It never really did. Thirty years later, I've come to accept that I don't quite fit in the deaf world. I don't know sign language; I went to mainstream schools, where I was usually the only kid with a disability; and I have never been a part of Deaf culture. As for the hearing world? Well, it isn't quite sure what to do with me, either.

To compensate, I've tried to be as "normal" as possible. In elementary school, I discovered that if I didn't make my deafness a "thing," most other people wouldn't either. I learned to sit in the front row of classes so I wouldn't have to ask my teachers to repeat themselves. When my friends wanted to watch TV or go to the movies, I learned to suggest another, better activity, so I didn't have to admit that without closed-captioning, which was a rarity at the time, I wouldn't be able to understand what was going on. I learned to mirror the facial expressions of people so that even if I didn't understand what they were saying, they at least *thought* I did. I laughed at the right times and *uh-huh*ed when appropriate. I did things deaf people don't typically do, like play the saxophone in the high school marching band and go out for the cheerleading squad. I earned my doctorate and became a college professor, assuaging my students' fears on the first day of class by saying that if they could get past this voice coming out of me, they would learn a whole lot of important stuff.

But I was never really normal. I never learned the secret password.

And then something amazing and entirely unexpected happened: I discovered running. The first time I ran a 5K was the first time I really felt normal. No one knew—or cared—that I was deaf. My ears had nothing to do with what my legs were trying to accomplish. Shortly after, I started writing about running—first for blogs, then for national magazines, and then a book. At last, I had a voice—a normal voice—that didn't make people flinch!

It was great. Whereas before, people knew me as "the deaf one," now I had a whole bunch of folks who knew me only as Susan Lacke—the writer, the runner, sometimes even the funny one. My hearing aid faded into the background, becoming just as much a part of me as a kneecap or fingernail—something I don't think about very much, much less talk about.

But when I had to actually talk to people in the running world, that liberating feeling came to a screeching halt. At a race, for example, I'd meet readers in person and see the change in their expression within the first 15 seconds of our conversation. As they looked me up and down, I felt them taking me in: *That body. That finishing time. That voice. That hearing aid.* "Oh, wow," they'd say. "I didn't know you were . . ."

What came next really stung: "You're a *runner*?"

There it was. I was still different. I didn't really belong in the running club. It was "supercalifragilistic" all over again.

I've discovered that I wasn't the only one who felt this way. Many runners deal with a kind of impostor syndrome, feeling as though they don't belong in the sport. You can spot them fairly easily—they are always quick to let you know they're a runner but that they're not a "real runner."

I was certainly guilty of this. I would rarely speak to others about my race plans, and when I did, I'd often minimize them. "It's *only* a 5K," I'd be quick to point out, shaking my head. Or, "It's not like I'm going to win or anything." If someone congratulated me on a marathon or triathlon finish, I'd laugh: "Oh, come on. I was bringing up the caboose of that train. They gave me a medal because they felt sorry for me." When I was introduced as someone who wrote for a running magazine, I'd try to beat them to the punch line. "I know, I know, I'm a fluke," I'd say. "I'm still waiting for my boss to figure out I don't know what I'm doing."

But secretly, in my heart of hearts, I wanted to be a "real runner." I wanted to fit the mold of what people expected of me as someone who writes about running. I wanted to have the lean physique and fast finishing times of the people on the covers of the magazine I write for. I wanted to not feel like a fraud.

So I decided to train. I mean, really train. I mustered up the courage to ask my magazine editor for coaching. Mario Fraioli, or "Coach Dude" as I came to call him, had coached Olympian runners and marathon champions. He wrote all the training plans for the magazine. If anyone knew the secret password, it was him; if anyone could make someone a "real" runner, it would be him.

He asked what my goal was. I said it was to qualify for the Boston Marathon. That definitely seemed like a goal a real runner would have.

"Hmm, okay," he said. "What's your current marathon PR?"

I told him. It was exactly an hour off what I would need to even get my foot in the door for Boston.

"Get me there?" I pleaded. It was a big ask, I knew that.

But he agreed to try. "Let's do this," he said.

It would be awesome if what followed were a montage of kick-ass hill repeats, blazing track workouts, and my great attitude. I would love it if the highlight reel contained me getting slimmer and faster as Coach Dude blows a whistle in my face and cracks the proverbial whip. At the climax, I would triumphantly cross the finish line at the exact time I needed to qualify for the Boston Marathon. Coach Dude would hug me and, with a tear running down his cheek, say he was so proud. I'd know the password, and finally—*finally!*—I'd be a real runner. I'd even change my byline in the magazine: "Susan Lacke, Real Runner."

What actually happened? Not that. I followed Coach Dude's training plan diligently, but many days, it felt all but impossible. Yet when he asked how things were going, I'd say, "Great!" and ask for more. I knew I couldn't handle it, but I also knew a real runner could. So until I became one, I was going to fake it. Coach Dude, who lived 500 miles away and was coaching me remotely, had to take my word for it.

Things started to hurt; I kept running. My asthmatic lungs got angry; I doubled up on my medicine and kept running. I was hungry all the time, but I knew real runners were lean. So I ate a rice cake and tried to convince myself that no, I actually *really like* rice cakes!

When I rolled my ankle on a hike with my husband, Neil, I limped home on a big purple foot. I told Coach Dude I needed the day off. The next day, I wrapped up my swollen limb, shoved it into a running shoe, and pushed on.

Though my ankle eventually returned to its normal size, a stinging sensation in the joint remained. From time to time, my ankle would even give out from under me mid-stride, sending me tumbling. And still, I ran. I didn't tell anyone, even Coach, what was really going on. My ability to run through injury became like a silent point of pride. Real runners are tough, right? A few weeks later, I ran a half-marathon and set a PR. This was working!

Then one morning, my alarm clock buzzed to kick me out of bed for a scheduled early-morning run. I hit the button, groaned, and set my foot on the floor.

What the . . . ? My ankle refused to move. When I tried to flex my foot at the joint, it was locked. I couldn't get a pair of shoes on, much less run. I slid on a pair of flip-flops and went to my doctor.

Soon after—in fact, the very day I was scheduled to pick up my race packet for my Boston-qualifying marathon, the entry-way to my becoming a "real" runner—I was in an MRI tube, trying to find out what was going on with my ankle.

"Well, what is it?" I asked, peering anxiously over my doctor's shoulder as he scrolled through my results on a computer screen. I didn't like the look of his knitted brow.

"What I'm trying to figure out here," he finally said, turning to look me in the eye, "is whether your pain tolerance is just that high or you're just that stubborn."

As it turned out, rolling my ankle had fractured it in two places and torn a ligament. Ankle reconstruction surgery was scheduled, and racing plans were shelved. They rebroke my ankle to set it correctly and then cut deep into the joint to repair my ligament. All of it hurt less than the blow to my ego.

Even as my ankle slowly healed and I returned to running and triathlons, one thing after another kept me from trying for Boston again. My best friend, Carlos, who had inspired me to take up running in the first place, passed away from cancer. Losing him also meant losing my fount of inspiration and motivation. At that same time, I moved to a new city, where I struggled to adjust and assimilate. I was lonely, so I took on more writing work to feel some kind of connection with humanity, even if it was just Facebook comments and tweets on an article or column I wrote.

Through it all, there remained this unfinished business of becoming a real runner. It gnawed at me on a daily basis. I started covering miles just for the sake of covering miles. With no real plan and waning motivation, I found myself going through the motions, doing the things runners are supposed to do. I signed up for local races. I bought fancy new gear. I choked down gels at 45-minute intervals. I was running the miles, but it had all become so mechanical and uninspired. Neil, an endurance athlete himself, began to look at me with concern as I returned home disenchanted from another lackluster run.

I signed up for yet another race—the Huntsville Marathon in Utah—hoping that this time, things would somehow click, my hard work would pay off, and I would finish the race and feel transformed. Yet when I crossed the finish line, I felt exactly the same. Nothing had changed.

"You did it!" Neil said cheerily, wrapping his arms around me outside the finishing chute. "You set a new PR!" This was true—

I had run that marathon 9 minutes faster than my previous personal best. But rather than feeling elation, I thought, *Yeah, but I'm still too slow for Boston.*

I looked at Neil and shrugged: "Let's go." I didn't even want to stay for the post-race buffet. All I wanted was to get as far away from the finish line as fast as possible. I just didn't give a shit about any of it anymore.

"What happened?" Neil asked as we drove home from the race. "You usually love race day!"

I just stared out the window in silence.

I had always loved race day because I felt like I belonged, but somehow, somewhere along the way, I had stopped feeling that way. Now, every time I toed the line, I would look at the runners surrounding me like they were part of some other tribe. They looked so fit. They looked so ready. They looked so excited. They knew the secret password. I didn't.

"Maybe marathons just aren't your thing," Neil said with a shrug.

I frowned and shook my head. "Marathons have to be my thing."

"Do they really?" he asked. "I figured you'd know better by now."

"What is that supposed to mean?" I said, glaring at him.

"There's more than one way to be a runner, isn't there?" Neil replied. "You write all kinds of stories about all kinds of runners. So I guess the question is, what kind of runner are you?"

I didn't know what to say. I sulked the rest of the drive home because I didn't have an answer. I sulked because I wanted so badly to have one. But I mostly sulked because I really, *really* didn't want to admit Neil was right.

Had I been so hung up on some arbitrary goal that I had lost sight of what running actually meant to me? Was there more to running than just getting faster or finishing a certain race? Was there even such a thing as being a "real" runner, and if so, would I ever feel like one? What was the secret password?

I didn't know—but I was sure as hell going to find out.

IN DEFENSE OF
3:00 A.M. REGISTRATIONS

I REALLY SHOULD NOT BE ALLOWED to operate electronic devices after midnight.

If you look at my email history, you'll see most of my race registrations are time-stamped with ungodly hours: My first 5K registration was completed shortly after midnight on New Year's Day; my first half-marathon, at 3:21 a.m.; my first triathlon, 4:09 in the morning. Some people watch late-night infomercials, some raid the fridge for a midnight snack—I click the "Register" button.

It was yet another tussle with insomnia that kicked off my quest to rediscover my identity as a runner. The night after Neil called me out at the Huntsville Marathon, I tossed and turned as his words rolled around in my head.

What kind of runner are you? I thought.

Once upon a time, I had had an answer to that question. When I first started running, I was up for just about anything. Every weekend was another race—a costumed 5K with a friend, a splash-and-dash race with Neil, a trail run with beautiful vistas. Whether I ran well or finished dead last, I loved the excited butterflies in my stomach at the start and the growing confidence I felt with every finish line crossed. I craved the taste of a hard-earned beer in the trailhead parking lot or a sinful trip through the drive-through for French fries and milkshakes on the ride home.

But what I really loved was registering for a race. These decisions were rarely made impulsively. Rather, I'd hear about a race, pull up the website on the computer, wonder if I could do it, and then ultimately determine that I could not. An hour later, I'd revisit, wondering if I was being silly. *Surely it couldn't be that hard.* Then I'd change my mind. *It's definitely too challenging, I don't have the right training, people will laugh at me.* I'd close out the race website on my laptop and walk away.

Midnight would roll around, and I'd find myself still thinking about it. By 1:00 a.m., I'd be sitting in the darkness, illuminated only by the light of my screen, finger hovering over the

"Register" button. I wasn't on the race website because of insomnia; it was the other way around—the insomnia was caused by the race. A new distance or bigger challenge was so exciting, it kept me up at night.

"Screw it," I'd say to myself, usually out loud. "I'm in."

Click.

It's so easy to be bold in the darkness.

When morning came, proof of my questionable decision-making would be right there at the top of my inbox: Congratulations! You are now registered to have your ass handed to you at the most mountainous of marathons! What the hell were you thinking?!?

Research has shown why this happens. Sleep deprivation, even in minor doses, causes increased brain activity in the regions that process optimism, while suppressing the areas of the brain that evaluate consequences. It's the reason casinos remove their clocks and black out their windows—the later you stay up, the more likely you are to push in all your chips on a risky hand.

In the dark of night, the registration thought process boils down to *How bad could it be, really? I'm in!* But the morning light reveals more than a bank deduction for race fees. Now you have to run the damn thing. The optimism fades away, and panic sets in. A funny thing happens when it comes to these bad decisions, though—they sometimes end up being the smartest things you've ever done. There's something spectacular about setting a goal beyond your current abilities: It scares you into doing the work.

And for that, I was always grateful.

Too often, we're told to think things through. "Sleep on it," reasonable people say. "Don't make a dumb decision." Caution is praised over chutzpah, but I'm not sure that's always a good thing. Caution can make people overestimate risk and shrink from opportunities. It can make us close out the computer screen and focus on goals we perceive as more reasonable. Caution is safe. Caution is wise. Caution is really, really boring.

Years ago, I thought I was being bold by trying to qualify for the Boston Marathon. It was an ambitious goal and a worthy one for many runners. However, it wasn't *my* goal. I had aimed for it because I thought I was supposed to. If I wanted to be taken seriously as a runner and writer in the endurance sports space, I reasoned, it was a box I needed to check.

But was it, really?

I wrestled with that question as I stared into the darkness at 1:00 a.m. the night after the Huntsville race. When was the last time I had looked at a race website and felt those butterflies? It had been a while. My brain scrolled through my time line as an endurance athlete, trying to determine when I had last felt excited about running.

I recalled how, years ago, I had been tempted to run an ultramarathon, but knowing I was probably too slow to make any of the cutoff times, I had dismissed that idea quickly. And as someone who writes about endurance sports, I would often hear about offbeat races around the world: a naked 5K in Tampa or a race in England where participants chase a wheel of cheese down a hill. These were certainly not what I thought of as "real" running events, but they sure looked like a blast. And Coach Dude had just run all the way across the Grand Canyon for fun. That wasn't even a race at all, although, man, it looked stunning. But I couldn't handle a run of that magnitude, could I?

All these thoughts swirled around in my head that night. *No, this was impossible.* I closed my eyes and tried to sleep. *I'll deal with it in the morning. Or never.*

But at 2:00 a.m., there I was, sitting in the darkness, illuminated by the glow of my computer screen. Neil rolled over groggily. "What are you doing, babe?" he mumbled. I shushed him, patting his back to assure him he had nothing to worry about.

On my screen, I had more than a dozen browser tabs open, each with a different running experience. With some careful planning, I could spend an entire year doing new races, different races, races that excited me, and races that flat-out scared me. Just the thought of it gave me the butterflies I had been missing for far too long.

"Screw it," I said out loud. "I'm in." Before I could change my mind, I was clicking the "Register" button again and again.

I woke up the next morning, my laptop still open on my chest. Congratulations! You are now registered to have your ass handed to you for the next 365 days! I had pushed all my chips in.

If I wanted to win this hand, I had best put my shoes on and get to work.

IT'S ALL
UPHILL FROM HERE

THE WINNING TIME for this 400-meter dash was 3 minutes, 58 seconds.

If that sounds slow for a distance where record-breaking times are measured in seconds, not minutes, blame it on the altitude—after all, the starting line of this race is situated at a wind-sucking 6,780 feet above sea level, and the finish line is located at 7,308 feet. To get from Point A to Point B, athletes must run up a ski jump built for the 2002 Winter Olympics. To be plain, that's 528 vertical feet of climbing in just 400 meters (or, as most of us would call it, "a wall").

The Red Bull 400 is not a fast event. It's not a place to knock out a few easy hill repeats. And it's decidedly *not* for people with sound decision-making skills. Let's face it, nothing about sprinting up a ski jump is logical or smart. When my editors assigned me to cover the event a few years back, I'll be honest—I shook my head and muttered something about "sadistic wackjobs." But I also had to admit, I was curious. What kind of person willingly *does* a race like this?

The more I thought about it, the more I wasn't sure if watching from the sidelines would be the best way to understand an event as seemingly nutty as this one. More important, I needed to understand the sadistic wackjobs who did it.

"I'm thinking about signing up for the race to see what it's really like," I told my editor.

"You're out of your mind," he replied. "You'll roll right back down the hill before you even start!"

And just like that, my curious tendrils shrank back. Yep, he was absolutely right. It was a dumb idea. The wise thing to do would be to simply *report* on the people who lacked logic and smarts, not actually be one. So that year, I ventured out to the K120 Nordic ski jump in Park City, Utah, solely as an observer of this asshattery.

Ski jumps are designed for maximum speed going downhill. When you go the opposite direction . . . well, you get the opposite effect. From the first wave of the Red Bull 400, it was obvious that this wasn't a normal hill run. For starters, most hills don't have rope netting attached to keep you from falling backward. They also don't have oxygen masks stationed every 100 meters.

"Has anyone needed to use that yet?" I asked a medic carrying a tank of oxygen to the summit.

"Not yet," he smiled. (Did I detect a hint of sadism?) "But give it time." (Yes, I did.)

And they would need it all right, of that I was certain. As I talked with the nervous racers awaiting their wave starts, one thing became very clear, very quickly: Most of the runners weren't runners at all. For many, this was the first and only running event they planned to do in their lifetime. Some of the competitors were Winter Olympians-in-training who spent their days going down the ski jump and who were curious as to what it'd be like to go up. Others were gym-rat enthusiasts looking for an epic challenge. Some—mostly college students, it seemed—simply signed up on a double dog dare. Encountering someone with a traditional road-running pedigree at the Red Bull 400 was a rarity.

Curious to know how someone went about preparing for a race like this, I struck up a conversation with a young woman from Salt Lake City, waiting for her turn to race. I asked her whether she'd done lots of hill repeats or perhaps some lower-body strength sessions at the gym. She pursed her lips and shook her head: "Mostly, I just prayed a lot."

"Solid strategy," I replied, before gesturing toward the ski jump. "Your wave starts soon. Have you thought about what it might be like to run up that?"

"I'm trying not to think about it, actually," she said pointedly. "Can we talk about something else?"

Ah, denial. Seeing that this interview wasn't going to get very far, I wished her luck and headed to the steep metal staircase that ascended along the side of the ski jump. On the way up, I crossed paths with racers coming down the stairs after finishing. Their weakened legs visibly vibrated with every step, as if they might buckle at any second.

"How was it?" I asked one of the racers passing by, a red-faced guy in basketball shorts and a checkered pair of hipster skateboarding shoes.

"Awesome!" he yelled, raising his hand in the air for a high five. The action was rescinded quickly when he realized that holding the handrail was the only thing keeping him upright.

I finally made it to the top of the staircase, breathing hard, and stopped to chat with a guy from Kentucky, who shook his head and had just one word for the race: "Brutal." A track-and-field athlete from Utah State University described the 400 as "similar pain, just in different muscles" compared to his specialty, the mile. A woman from Park City said it was the hardest thing she had ever done. And these were the people who were upright. Most just moaned while curled into a fetal position.

"All I could think was, 'Shoot me now,'" gasped one competitor, doubled over with her hands on her knees as she tried to catch her breath. "About three-quarters of the way up, I wanted to quit so bad."

"So why didn't you?"

"I was scared to let go of the rope! It's a long way down."

And so it went, wave by wave, as finishers went from vertical to horizontal the second they crossed the finish line. The oxygen masks were put to good use, as were the many puke buckets.

"That sucked," they moaned.

"I hurt so bad," they cried.

"I'm totally coming back next year," they laughed breathlessly.

When I wrote my article on the race, I suggested that maybe the people who signed up were a few tacos short of a combination platter. After all, who would be nuts enough to spend a Saturday morning running *up* a ski jump? Don't they know it's much easier the other way around? Haven't these dumbasses heard of gravity? Why would a bunch of gym goers and audacious college kids sign up for a race that even runners knew was too hard?

But I had to admit that I admired those dumbasses. The most surprising thing about the Red Bull 400 was not that hundreds of people were stupid enough to do it. The most surprising thing was that they *loved* it. Not one person I talked to said they regretted their decision to enter the race. They were all so . . . satisfied. Tired, quivering, and vomitrocious, yes, but still very satisfied—joyful, even. Beneath all my snarky comments, the truth was that I envied them.

I wanted to know what that kind of satisfaction felt like. I wanted to face my fears and come out on the other side, gobsmacked and smiling.

So when it came time to sign up for races outside my comfort zone, this one immediately came to mind. If I planned to spend the next 365 days doing races that scared me, then running up an Olympic ski jump was the perfect way to find out if I really had the courage to follow through on my plan.

But it was one thing to register for the race—that was the easy part, I learned, as I filled out the entry blank. Actually doing it was something else altogether. What if I didn't have the gumption?

"I don't know why you're so scared," Neil said, discerning my panic on the night before the race. "It's just a few minutes of your life. It's not like it's an Ironman® or anything."

"Easy for you to say," I retorted, glaring at him. "You're not the one doing it."

It was absolutely clear from what I'd seen the year prior that just a few minutes of this race had the potential to inflict more pain than an hours-long triathlon. I prefer my suffering in a slow, manageable trickle. To experience all the pain at once, even if briefly, sounded terrifying. I sputtered out all the what-ifs: What if I hurt myself tumbling down the ski jump? What if the conditions were too much for my asthma? *What if I died?*

"Died?" Neil looked highly skeptical.

"It could happen!" I hissed. "Those oxygen masks aren't for decorative purposes, you know."

The next morning, as I stumbled out of bed and into the kitchen for a cup of coffee, I was surprised to find Neil scurrying around the house, stuffing items into a backpack: gloves, a hat, my asthma inhaler.

"Drink up," he said, gesturing to my coffee mug. "We're leaving in 10 minutes."

"What?" This was unexpected. "I thought you had to go to work today."

"I told them I'd be coming in a little late," he said, placing his camera into the backpack. "I'm going to make sure you don't chicken out."

If gumption failed, my husband was ready to step in. I peered into his bag, half-expecting to see a cattle prod in his gear collection.

The drive to Park City was tense. Neil tried to reassure me that all would be fine, but I shushed him midsentence. When he tried to give me a pep talk, I halted that, too.

"Can we just talk about something else?" I pleaded. I planned to ride a wave of denial all the way to the starting line. This denial involved deluding myself that no, we were not driving to a sufferfest on a ski jump—rather, we were heading to Saturday morning brunch, like normal people. Smart people. People with pancakes.

When we arrived, the race was already in full swing, with early waves of the men's and women's races scampering (albeit slowly) up the jump every 15 minutes. Medics were replenishing the supply of oxygen tanks and puke buckets, lugging them up the stairs to the summit. An early-season frost had fallen on the mountain town overnight, dusting the already slick surface of the ski jump with an extra layer of slip-and-slide. My cold toes stiffened in my running shoes. My asthmatic cough flared up in the bracing air.

Nope. No way.

I did an abrupt about-face and started heading straight back to the car. Neil quickly put his arm around my shoulders and turned me back around.

"Your wave starts in 10 minutes," he said, unflinching. "Let's get you to the start line." I reluctantly obliged, just in case he really did have a cattle prod in his bag.

As we made our way toward the starting corral, pushing through the crowd of spectators gathered at the bottom of the ski jump, I couldn't help but notice the exuberance of the finishers returning to their friends and families.

"DUDE!" one racer bellowed as his friends gathered around him. "That was insane!" He recapped the climb, gesticulating wildly. "It starts out flat, and then . . . oh, man, it's so NOT!" It was so hard he couldn't breathe, he said, but he made it to the top. His friends hooted and slapped his back in celebration. Their friend was a bona fide badass.

I wanted someone to slap my back like that. Hell, I wanted to slap my own back. I really wanted to feel that same kind of post-race joy and satisfaction. With this reminder of why I was doing this race in the first place, my nerves gave way to excitement. Before I could change my mind, I turned to Neil with a smile and two thumbs up.

"I got this."

With butterflies in my stomach, I stepped into the starting corral just as the gun went off. In hindsight, that was the perfect way to start: no time to think, only do. I took off running with the 30 women in my wave—first on a flat 100-meter stretch of grass that led to the base of the ski jump and then the climb. And DUDE, the course description was accurate, all right. The Red Bull 400 starts out flat, and then . . . oh, man, it's so NOT.

The severity of the climb didn't hit me until about 200 meters in, when I discovered that I was no longer running but scrambling. When did that happen? Instead of pushing off on my toes, I was hanging on to the grid of ropes on the ground, clenching tightly until I found my footing on the slippery fake grass that covered the ski jump. At 250 meters, the course tapered, forcing participants to bottleneck into a narrow chute. Feet stepped on hands, hands slapped faces, and faces dripped with sweat.

My throat dried up as I sucked in air. As I struggled to swallow, a metallic taste suddenly coated my tongue, as if a penny had exploded in my mouth. I had heard of this phenomenon before but had never experienced it—during intense exercise in an anaerobic state, blood can leak into the lungs. The metallic taste comes from the iron content of the red blood cells.

It was official: I was dying. I just hoped that at my funeral, Neil would at least admit I was right: "She tried to tell me this could happen. I didn't listen to her. I'm an idiot." Amid the gasping and grabbing and hanging on for dear life, this hope gave me no small sense of satisfaction.

Then, suddenly, everything stopped. The wall of ropes and fake grass and human bodies gave way to open space, bright lights, and a giant blue mat.

"Good job!" a voice cheered as two hands grabbed me by the waist and pulled me off the ropes. I was carried away from the finish and led to where other competitors were sprawled out on the ground, gasping.

"Wait," I wheezed as the volunteer set me down and walked away to retrieve another runner. "That's *it*?"

The volunteer looked over his shoulder, an amused smile on his face. "Yeah, that's it," he chuckled.

It took a few minutes for my wheezing breaths to calm and a few more minutes for the metallic taste in my mouth to dissipate. But the bewilderment lingered for hours. I made my way down the stairs on wobbly legs, trying to piece together exactly what had happened. The race was flat, and then it wasn't, and then it was . . . over? Those 400 meters, even on a steep incline, had gone by so quickly. To be honest, I had been expecting much worse. Was it possible I had blown the race out of proportion? Was it possible I had underestimated my own fitness and abilities? Was it possible I was actually a badass after all? A smile slowly crept across my face.

"How'd it go?" Neil asked excitedly, as he jogged up the stairs to meet me.

"I . . . I thought . . . it would be harder." It felt strange to say that out loud.

Neil laughed. "I know. You do this every time."

I stopped walking and looked quizzically at him. "What do you mean?"

"You psych yourself out every time you do a new race," he continued. "Remember your first marathon? Your friends had to lock you out of the car so you would get on the start-line shuttle."

He extended his hand and helped me down the stairs as he recited a litany of my racing freak-outs over the years: the flustered texts I sent my mother before my first triathlon; the unflinching conviction that I would keel over while running my first trail race; the time he pushed me into the water before my first Ironman triathlon, because I was too paralyzed with fear to jump in. I had finished all those races, too, he reminded me.

"Haven't you learned by now?" Neil asked with a smile. "It's never as bad as you think it's going to be."

It was a timely reminder.

How many times had I learned this lesson? And how many times would I have to relearn it during my year of discomfort? So often, the hardest part of a race isn't getting to the finish line—it's showing up to the start in the face of all the fears and unknowns and what-ifs. Just about every new challenge sounds like a dumb decision at first. Some people have no business getting off the couch and training for a 5K, but they do it anyway.

The idea of running a marathon is preposterous to some people, until it's done. A hundred miles? Insane. Running up a ski jump or through a mud obstacle course or across the Grand Canyon? Irresponsible.

What if you hurt yourself? What if the conditions are too much? *What if you die?*

Yet there are millions of runners doing all those preposterous things and more, the what-ifs be damned. In fact, the unknown is a big part of the fun—not to mention, the reason for those wonderful butterflies.

Truth is, we're a lot more badass than we give ourselves credit for.

I thought the elated racers at the Red Bull 400 were satisfied because they were finished, but that wasn't it at all. The satisfaction came just from doing the damn thing. I didn't know the difference until I experienced it for myself. It's empowering to discover that the preposterous thing was actually possible all along. What other preposterous things are out there to conquer? If I don't show up, I'll never know.

Showing up sounds simple enough, but it takes a lot: a suspension of logic and smarts, an abundance of gumption, a good bit of denial, and sometimes, a little outside assistance to get us out of our own way. But the most important thing is to do the damn thing.

I walked away from the Red Bull 400 with satisfaction and a new mantra for my next race: *It's never as bad as you think it's going to be.* I had survived my first scary challenge in spite of myself. I felt ready for the year of challenges ahead.

But first, I was ready for brunch. A Saturday morning like this one definitely deserved some pancakes.

DAVY CROCKETT, DUST STORMS, AND A BAG FULL OF POOP

IT'S THE TRICK EVERY RUNNER FALLS FOR: If you can run a 5K, you can run a half-marathon. If you can run a half, you can run a full. Every time a finish line is crossed, the goalposts are moved, taunting runners to keep going.

It's not a lie. If someone can run 3.1 miles, adding 10 more miles to that isn't entirely out of reach. It takes training, sure, but it's not impossible. The fundamental truth of running is that if you can cover even 1 mile, it's within your power to run 10, 100, or even 1,000. "Impossible" goes out the window the first time a runner crosses a finish line.

Maybe that's why runners tumble so easily into that next big thing. A finish line is really just a starting line for the next goal. So, by that logic, if you can run a full, you can *definitely* do an ultramarathon, right? That was the dodgy reasoning that got me into the Pony Express 50-mile trail run.

For years, I'd admired the low-maintenance cool of ultrarunners. Unlike road racers, who have been known to wear pricey, color-coordinated outfits of moisture-wicking tech materials, ultrarunners often show up in mismatched socks and whatever clothes are clean that day, whether it's a free tech tee from a 1998 5K 'n' Vegan Potluck or a flannel shirt. Instead of obsessing over splits, they seem more interested in finding out what the view is like from the top of "that mountain over there." They eschew gels for cookies, stomp through mud puddles, and think nothing of stopping on the side of the trail to take a power nap. And they always have the most epic stories.

I have friends who have not only run 135 miles through California's Death Valley, but they have done so in the hottest part of July. When one friend came home from an ultramarathon in Hawaii, she shared the tale of being chased midrace by a wild boar through a dark, slick cave. While crewing at a 100-mile race in Colorado, I learned that one of the race leaders had gradually lost her vision in the final miles of the race, feeling her way through the trail's rocks, hairpin turns, and obstacles by touch alone.

Every ultrarunner I encountered would spin fantastic and outrageous tales of badassery that had me swooning. They really were the coolest.

"Oh, man," I would always say. "I wish I could do that."

And the reply, every time, was always the same: "Well, why don't you? If you can run a marathon, you can do an ultra."

Here's the ultra-math: If one can run a 26.2-mile marathon at an 8-minute-per-mile pace, that person already has the fitness to cover double the distance at a slower pace—say, 10 minutes per mile. In an ultra, walk breaks, especially on beastly uphills, are not a sign of weakness but a smart strategy. The most common advice you'll hear from ultrarunners is to start slow and get slower.

"Ultrarunning isn't racing in a lung-busting, leg-burning sense of the word," my ultrarunning friend Jason told me. "It's more like jogging with a soft *j*. Yogging."

But there was one major flaw with this plan: I was already pretty slow. My marathon pace would leave most runners wondering if I was already yogging it in. There was no way I could make the cutoff of any ultramarathon. Whenever I thought of doing an ultra, I envisioned arriving at mile 50 of a race in the pitch black of night, the finish line already disassembled.

Or so I thought. When I actually took the time to visit the website for the Pony Express Trail 50, however, one of the first lines proved me wrong: There is a 19.5-hour cutoff for 50-mile finishers. This is very doable. We have had many finishers who were more than 60 years old.

With that, the only excuse I had disappeared. A cutoff of 19.5 hours? I could conceivably walk 50 miles in that time, if it came to that. (I *really* hoped it wouldn't come to that.)

The Pony Express Trail 50 takes place on a stretch of the historic letter-carrying route in the Middle of Nowhere, Utah. The start line was located on lands so remote, my GPS couldn't even find the location. I had to rely on written directions from the race director, which were almost entirely void of particulars, save the last bit of instruction: "If you reach the town of Vernon, you've gone too far."

That's the kind of folksy advice one could expect from a guy named Davy Crockett. (And, yes, that is his real name.) Davy Crockett founded the Pony Express Trail 50 and 100 in 2006 with only five runners, who thought it'd be fun to say they "ran in the hoofprints of history." He was a local ultrarunning legend known for a no-frills approach to racing. Aid stations at the Pony Express were nonexistent. Runners supplied their own crew, food, and water. The start line was a string of Christmas lights connected to a car battery. Oh, and there would be no porta-potties along the 50-mile, point-to-point course. This was the Wild West.

Unlike other races I had done, with their over-the-top expos featuring table loads of shiny, new gear, the Pony Express expo scene was, in a word, understated. There were no smiling volunteers coaxing me inside or pre-race talks or free samples of nutrition products. Instead, there was a white beach canopy that looked like it could blow away at any minute, and beneath it sat one Davy Crockett, checking runners' names off a short registration list.

"Here's your T-shirt and WAG bag," Crockett said, tossing a shiny metallic package across the table without looking up. "Start's in five minutes."

"WAG bag?" I asked, thinking he must mean SWAG bag, the runner's shorthand for "stuff we all get" at packet pickup. But Davy Crockett had already moved on to the next runner. There was no time to explain; the start was in five minutes.

I read the label on the bag: It said WAG, all right—as in Waste Alleviation and Gelling. This odor-tight, resealable foil package contained beads that turned liquid waste into solid for hygienic, spill-proof transport. Because there were no porta-potties along the course, runners were required to follow the "pack it in, pack it out" rule for waste of all kinds.

In other words, I was expected to shit in a bag.

"No one warned me about this," I said, showing the bag to Neil, who was manning my crew vehicle for the day. Neil suppressed the urge to gag.

"I love you, babe," Neil said with great hesitation, "but I'm not touching your poop bag."

I didn't have time to discuss the logistics of my WAG bag's transport. Davy Crockett and his megaphone were summoning runners to the start-line string of Christmas lights. It was

5:00 a.m., and the sun wouldn't be up for another two hours. With a 10-second countdown, Crockett sent off 20 or so yoggers, headlamps bobbing into the darkness.

Because it's a historic route, the Pony Express Trail is well maintained. The wide dirt road was even and without potholes. I was grateful for that as the pack of runners disappeared into the darkness ahead of me, leaving me to navigate the path with a single beam of light from my headlamp. Once in a while, a crew car would pass, briefly lighting up the trail and giving me a glimpse of what was ahead—mostly dirt, though occasionally I'd see a runner squatting behind a desert shrub on the side of the road, presumably using their WAG bag.

It was up to runners to determine the frequency of their crew stops. I had asked Neil to meet me first at mile 10, a checkpoint I reached just as the sun was breaking over the horizon.

"How do you feel?" Neil asked, refilling the hydration backpack I was carrying as I applied sunscreen to my cheeks.

"Pretty good, I think," I replied. "Should I be going faster?"

"Nah," Neil replied. "You're doing fine."

"Am I in last place, though?" I was certain I already knew the answer. Despite the long, flat stretch of the Pony Express Trail, I hadn't seen another runner ahead of or behind me for at least 2 miles.

"You're doing fine," Neil repeated as he thrust the backpack into my hands and sent me on my way with a playful pat on the bottom. "Now giddy up, horsey!"

I handed him my headlamp. "See you at mile 20?"

Neil smiled. "Count on it."

The car disappeared in a cloud of dust, and I ticked off the next 10 miles without seeing another soul. The thought of running the entire 50 miles by myself felt daunting. In a road marathon, I'd usually be surrounded by people, some running and some cheering from the sidelines. Here, I had only the desert shrubbery that lined the trail. The terrain was unchanging, as was the landscape.

"Hmph," I grunted at a prairie dog who had popped his head out from his burrow. "So much for epic stories, huh?"

To pass the time, I talked—to myself, to the shrubs, to the rocks in the road. I talked about why I was doing this and why this might have been a dumb idea. I talked about what I would do if I really came in last place or if I ended up missing the cutoff time after all. When I ran out of things to talk about, I listed the 50 states in alphabetical order and then the 50 states in alphabetical order along with their capital cities: *Alabama, Montgomery. Alaska, Juneau. Arizona, Phoenix . . .*

As promised, Neil was waiting for me at mile 20, and this time he had a peanut butter sandwich. I was glad to see him, not just for the sandwich but also for the company.

"I've started talking to myself," I confessed. "And to prairie dogs. I might actually go crazy by the end of this race."

"That's cute," Neil said, pushing a hat onto my head and giving me a kiss. "You think you weren't crazy before you started?"

Crew insolence? Absolutely. But hey, you take what you can get out there. I gave him a high five and headed back out.

At mile 26.2, my watch buzzed. I was officially entering the Great Unknown. I had never run more than a marathon before, and I honestly had no idea what to expect.

"Well, Self," I sighed, as I slowed to a walk. "How are we doing?" I took stock of my body and determined that I was actually doing pretty well. I was shocked. The only thing I had ever known was the heaviness of a marathon's final miles, when my legs only worked because my brain lied to them with promises of "only one more mile" for the last three miles. It was foreign to reach that same point and feel like I could keep going—possibly forever. It inspired a kind of awe I hadn't felt in years, a reverence for how incredibly fortunate I was to have this body that does the boneheaded things I ask of it.

"It's pretty cool, isn't it?" I said out loud, turning my face to the right.

"Damn straight it is," I replied, turning my face to the left and nodding in affirmation.

I chuckled as I resumed a yogging pace. Maybe Neil was right about me being crazy after all.

I finally spotted life at mile 28. A volunteer was driving the course, alerting runners to the possibility of a storm passing through. In the distance, I could see that dark clouds were forming, and I started to get excited about the idea of rain cleaning off my salt-crusted skin.

"Well, it's not quite rain . . . ," the volunteer replied at my observation. "More like dirt."

The National Weather Service was warning of 45-mile-per-hour winds moving in our direction, he said, and those winds were picking up desert dirt along the way. A wall of thick dust was barreling toward our exact location.

I didn't know what to make of this information. "So . . . ," I ventured, "this means the race is canceled?"

The volunteer laughed and shook his head. "This must be your first ultra."

At mile 30, I told Neil about the impending dust storm. As I lathered myself into a frenzy over what was to come, Neil calmly refilled my hydration backpack and handed it back to me.

"You said you wanted an epic story," Neil said, as he gestured in the direction of the dark, ominous storm in the distance. "Pretty sure you're about to get one."

The winds picked up shortly after Neil drove off to our next meeting point, his taillights vanishing into a wall of dust. The sun disappeared, and the temperature dropped suddenly, causing my skin to erupt in goose bumps. Before I could process what was going on, sand began lifting off the ground, peppering my face with tiny pebbles. A forceful gale howled as it blew through in gusts, pushing me sideways off the trail. There were no trees to hide behind, no place to take shelter. I pulled my shirt collar over my nose and pushed the brim of my hat down low over my eyes to block out the dirt.

The storm howled on and on as I leaned into the wind, barely able to see the trail in front of me. I could make out the faint glow of red lights blinking ahead. Was that Neil? I forged ahead, only to discover a pack of runners taking shelter from the wind behind an SUV. One of them reached out and pulled me by the arm, enfolding me in the pack.

No words were said; none were needed. We just stood there for what felt like forever, in a huddled mass, squinting to protect our eyes from the stinging artillery of sand. The wind was relentless, kicking up even more dirt around our cluster of bodies. When a tumbleweed hit the other side of the SUV with a loud *smack!*, I jumped, flinching as if it had hit my own skin.

And then, as suddenly as the wind had started, it ceased. It was as if a mother had walked into a room where her children were wrestling and yelled, "STOP THAT!" Everyone and everything froze. Dirt and debris dropped to the ground. We looked at each other, totally bewildered.

"What the hell just happened?" we whispered, as if we were scared the storm would hear us and return. One runner, pointing into the distance at another wall of dirt on its way, advised us to wait.

Reader, I should be embarrassed to admit this, but all I could think of in that moment was *I'm not in last place! Now is my chance!* And coming winds be damned, I took off running. Even as I took those first steps, I knew it was a bad idea. Still, I wondered if this was a sign from the Endurance Gods—a fresh opportunity to play catch-up. I ran on, determined to get to Neil at mile 40 before the next wave of dust hit.

I made it all of half a mile. But just as the winds began to push me around again, I saw another pair of blinking taillights—another shelter from the storm! I leaned into the fierce headwind, just trying to make it to the vehicle.

"Get in!" Neil yelled. The vehicle was ours! He had parked before mile 40, worried about the storm. I had never been so relieved to see my husband. I ran around to the passenger-side door and began pulling on the handle.

"It's locked!" I pointed at the door. Neil shook his head. I pulled on the door again, pleading with him to unlock it. Finally, after a heavy yank, the door gave a little bit. It wasn't locked after all—the wind was just so strong, it was blowing the door shut. Dismayed, I ran to Neil's side of the car, where he opened his door and let me scramble clumsily over his lap into the passenger seat.

The wind roared around our parked vehicle, rocking it with every gust. I tried to speak, to tell Neil what it had been like out there, but when I opened my mouth, only a loud wail came out. I had felt so good just 3 miles before—invincible, even. And now? Not so much. The sheer effort of making it those 3 miles had totally sapped my energy.

I started crying. "I don't think I can finish this," I sobbed. "It's too much."

I turned to look at Neil. He was clearly trying to suppress a laugh.

"You think this is funny?" I demanded, gesturing at the storm outside.

"No, that isn't funny," Neil said, biting his lower lip to keep from grinning. "But your face is."

I flipped down the car's sun visor and looked into the mirror. I started crying even harder: Every surface, from the hat on my head to the skin of my neck, was covered in thick, chalky dust—all except for two rivulets caused by the tracks of my tears.

Neil busted out laughing. "I'm sorry," he said, "but that's pretty epic."

It didn't feel epic. It felt freaking hard. I had signed up for a 50-mile run, not a cage fight with Mother Nature. I couldn't do this. And anyway, I wasn't an idiot, you know, I told Neil. Surely the rational people were dropping out of the race.

"Tell you what," Neil said gently. "Before you make any final decisions, drink this." He reached into the backseat and fished out an ice-cold can of cola from a cooler.

I began to tear up again. Neil may think I'm crazy, but when he does stuff like this, I know he really loves me.

After "start slow and get slower," the second-most common advice one hears in ultrarunning is: "Eating is the answer." If you're tired, eat. If you're slowing down, eat. If you're being an irritable pissy pants, eat. If you're crying, eat. After almost a decade of us training and racing together, Neil had come to recognize the warning signs that a bonk was imminent. My crying was a big tell that my blood sugar was dropping rapidly.

God bless caffeinated sugar water. Through cold soda, I can do all dumb things. By the time I finished the drink, I had started to think rationally again.

"Okay, I'm gonna try to run," I said, using Neil's shirt sleeve to wipe the tears and dirt off my face. The grime didn't faze him. He just looked at me proudly.

"Attagirl. I'll drive up a mile and meet you there."

I got out of the car and leaned into the wind. Yes, I could do a mile. I could do anything for a mile.

Neil met me up the road, just as he had promised. He opened the car door in case I wanted in.

"No," I said. "Another mile."

We leapfrogged through the course, a mile at a time, until the wind finally died down, the dust settled, and the sun shined brightly once more.

"I got this," I said to Neil at mile 40. "I'll see you at the finish."

I shared those last 10 miles with my fellow runners. Although I had surged ahead while others (smartly) stayed behind to take shelter during the storm, they eventually caught up to me and passed me. But by that time, I didn't care if I ended up in last place—I was going to finish! I was going to have an epic race story about the time I ran 50 miles! In a dust storm! And also, I pooped in a bag!

As it turns out, the reason ultrarunners have great stories is because a lot can happen over the course of 50 miles. Within the same race—even within the same mile—a lot can go horribly wrong, and a lot can go blissfully right. I found out after the race that all 22 starters in the 50-mile race, including 13 first-time ultrarunners, finished. All those rational people I thought were dropping out? Turns out they never existed. I suppose the fact that we all signed up for this race in the first place should have been a big hint.

If you can run a 5K, you can run a marathon. If you can run a marathon, you can run an ultra. The goalposts are always moving. As I stood in the shower after the race, watching the layers of dirt run off my skin and down the drain, I couldn't help but wonder just how far I could go under the power of my own two legs.

That night, at 3:00 a.m., awakened by a residual combination of adrenaline and caffeine, I fumbled for my phone on the nightstand. I needed to make an addition to my running calendar, STAT.

"What are you doing?" Neil muttered, awakened by the light of my phone screen.

"Signing up for a 24-hour race," I patted his arm reassuringly. "Go back to sleep."

Neil moaned softly, rolling over. "You're crazy."

"No," I grinned as I clicked the "Register" button. "I'm epic."

HOW DID I GET HERE?
AND WHERE ARE MY SHOES?

I AWOKE ON NEW YEAR'S DAY with the same thought as everyone else: *Where am I?*

This was followed by the other usual questions: *How did I get here? What time did I go to bed last night?* And, of course, everyone's favorite: *Where the hell are my shoes?*

But this was no champagne bender. This was Across the Years, and I had just run my way into a blackout.

I used to love New Year's. It was a time for jubilation and celebration, where we bid goodbye (and sometimes good riddance) to the past year and looked toward the future with optimism:

Next year will be better. It's a sentiment worthy of raising a champagne glass.

Trouble was, the champagne glass was by far my favorite part. New Year's was the one day of the year when staying up until after midnight and getting tipsy were not only accept-able but also encouraged! I didn't have that permission for the other 364 days a year, when "midnight" and "tipsy" were often replaced by blackouts and next-day Google searches for hang-over cures and Am I an alcoholic?

The answer to that question, by the way, was "Yes." More accurately: I was a drunk. The kind of drunk who poured a glass of wine before taking off her coat when she got home from work at 5:00 p.m. The kind of drunk who polished off the bottle by 7:00 p.m., still wearing her coat, and then stumbled to the store for more. The kind who woke up on the floor the next morning, asking, *Where am I?*

I drank to help quiet the nagging anxiety of the "Not Enoughs." Every time I did something, be it finishing a mara-thon, filing an article, or lecturing to a classroom of college stu-dents, I'd tend to see only my shortcomings. I was never quite good enough, charming enough, or eloquent enough. Instead of celebrating my accomplishments, my default setting was to find examples of people who did a better job than I did. A debilitat-ing by-product of the Not Enoughs was the constant fear that people would find out I was a fraud, that I would be outed for playing a very elaborate game of make-believe.

For that matter, I *was* playing an elaborate game of make-believe. When I lived alone, it was easy to keep my drinking a secret. But when Neil and I moved in together, maintaining the illusion of someone who has "just one glass of wine" to unwind at the end of the day took serious effort. I started leaving campus early, getting home before Neil, and downing a strong jump-start cocktail. I stayed up long after he went to bed, under the guise of grading papers, only to polish off the bottle and replace it with another one. I started hiding bottles around the house, taking swigs when he wasn't looking.

I thought I was doing a pretty convincing job, but there's an interesting thing about blackouts: They're selective. My last memory of a night might be saying, "I'm just going to stay up and grade these papers, honey." My brain would delete the part where I stumbled into the bedroom three hours later, turning on the lights to reveal a wine-stained shirt and a mascara-streaked face, which I pressed into the cheek of the man I loved, slurring: "Do you think I'm pretty?" It would also skip over the part where he asked, "Have you been drinking?" and I lied about it (unconvincingly). There's absolutely no memory of the argument that then ensued. And every time, I woke up the next morning, sleeping on the couch or the bathroom floor (or, one particularly confusing time, in the backseat of my car), and I wasn't sure how I got there.

It became very clear, very quickly, that I needed to do something. Like most alcoholics, I tried and failed, multiple times, to get my drinking under control. But the same thing that worked in my favor as an endurance athlete—a love for extremes and the high that comes when you find those extremes—worked against me in my attempts to have "just one." I finally had to admit that moderation wasn't possible. Whether it was riding a bike or drinking a box of wine, I didn't have wiring in my brain that allowed me to stop after just a little. Once I started, I had to squeeze every last drop out of the experience.

On August 1, 2012, I quit. I'd like to say this was the result of an epiphany or that I'd found some deep well of self-resolve, but the truth is that I woke up that morning, asking, "Where am I?" and quickly came to the terrifying realization that the answer was "in a pool of blood." At some point the previous night, after surpassing my self-imposed "just one glass" yet again, I had fallen and hit my head on a bookshelf. My first stop of the day was the emergency department. The second was to the home of a friend, who took me straight to my third stop—an Alcoholics Anonymous meeting. It was the worst day of my life and also the best: I'm still sober.

In my recovery, I've learned there's something that really does work in my favor both as an endurance athlete and in sobriety: I love a challenge. The part of my brain that chases the finish line is the same part that interprets the Alcoholics Anonymous adage of "one day at a time" as a dare. My daily routine is different in the quest for another 24 hours of sobriety—I go for a run after work, drink chamomile tea instead of wine, and successfully cross the finish line when I go to bed next to my husband. The best part? I wake up there, too. It's pretty rad.

That said, I thought that after I got sober, my days of blacking out were behind me. Across the Years proved me wrong.

I hadn't anticipated signing up for this race, although it had crossed my radar years ago, when I lived in Arizona. Across the Years is a legendary event on the Phoenix running scene, bridging the old year with the new via a fixed-time race, where runners cover as much ground as they can in 24, 48, 72, or 144 hours.

It wasn't the duration of the event that I found outrageous, nor was it the fact that the run took place on a 1-mile loop, repeated over and over. I didn't even think it was all that extreme to go for six days. After all, in a fixed-time race, runners can move as fast or as slow as they want and stop when they need to eat, change, or even sleep. It's not possible to take a DNF (or "did not finish") designation; runners can simply choose to stop for the day with the miles they have.

But running on New Year's Eve? Now that was crazy talk. Why ruin a perfectly good drinking holiday with a race? It didn't make sense. Even after I got sober, it never crossed my mind to enter Across the Years. I still relished the spirit of renewal that came with the holiday, but now I got my fill of hope and chamomile tea before going to bed by 10:00 p.m.

After finishing the Pony Express 50-miler, however, attempting Across the Years was the only thing I could think about.

If I wanted to know how far I could go, a 24-hour race was the perfect test of endurance. I was so excited, I didn't even mind when Neil pointed out to me that he wouldn't be able to crew for me because he had to work that night. No problem; I could handle this on my own.

"Look!" I exclaimed, showing him the website. "It says here I can just set up a tent on the loop. I'll take my gear, stash it in the tent, and make a pit stop when I need to replenish food and drinks."

"Can't you ask one of your friends in Phoenix to crew for you? I worry."

"It's not necessary," I said confidently, flicking my wrist in dismissal of his concern. "Besides, why would anyone want to give up their New Year's party to sit and watch me run laps around a park?"

"I don't know . . . ," Neil said hesitantly. "You're not great about staying on top of food and hydration. I don't see this ending well."

"Don't worry," I assured him. "It'll be fine." I believed it, too. After all, I used to pull all-nighters all the time when I drank. Surely, I could tap into that skill set while sober.

To save money on a hotel room, I traveled to Phoenix in the early-morning hours of New Year's Eve, arriving at Camelback Ranch just in time to set up my gear and supplies for the race. As I emptied my bag onto the floor of my small backpacking tent, a bright piece of paper fluttered out amid the gels and bottles of salt tablets. It was a note from Neil: *Don't forget to EAT!*

I laughed. He worried too much. With access to food at every mile, there was no way I'd have a problem fueling. I grabbed my bib number, zipped my tent, and headed for the start line.

"Susan? Is that you?" Someone tapped my shoulder.

"Cheryl!" I squealed. It was great to see a familiar face. Cheryl had been a friend since my time living in Phoenix, where we raced triathlon together. She was midway through her 48-hour race and was glad to see a new friend on the course. "Want some company?" I asked.

"You know it," she said. "I'm going for 100 miles. Come find me after you start." She jogged off around the bend of the course, her gait just as comfortable as if her race had just started.

I made it to the start line just in time to hear the race director's quick pre-race talk for the 24-hour runners. The rules were simple: Runners would alternate direction each hour in a clockwise and counterclockwise direction on the course. Cutting corners was not allowed. If a runner left the course to get supplies or to sleep in a tent or car, they had to return to the same spot and cross the next timing mat. Hot food offerings would be put out on the course every hour, thanks to volunteers who were delivering batches of pancakes, pots of homemade soup, and boxes of pizza.

"Also," the director said excitedly, "there's a party at midnight!" Everyone cheered uproariously. This was definitely going to be a fun way to ring in the new year.

An air horn sounded, and we 24-hour runners took off. With more than 200 people taking part in the event, there was no shortage of company on the course. I quickly made friends with a six-day racer named Bill.

"You're new!" Bill said excitedly as I jogged up alongside him. Over the course of six days, he made it a point to talk to every runner. With a kind, round face and a shock of white hair, Bill had a fun, grandfatherly personality that just about everyone made time to take in.

"I am!" I exclaimed, shaking his hand. "Got any advice for someone who's never done this before?"

"Yeah," he said. "Don't run so fast."

I laughed. Bill was in his 70s and had been running for a few days at that point. It was understandable that he'd be a little slower than me. Bill pushed his sunglasses down over his nose and peered over the top.

"No, I'm serious," he said. "It's a long race. Take it easy."

I smiled and let him know I appreciated the concern and that I'd catch up with him later. I continued on, striking up conversations with other runners and making more friends along the way. The laid-back atmosphere of the event made it easy to get to know one another, and 24 hours meant we had plenty of time to do so. As we discussed the sanity (or lack thereof) of marking New Year's with this event, a pattern emerged: Many of my fellow runners were using Across the Years as a replacement for all-night champagne binges.

Prior to Across the Years, my experience with this overlap was purely anecdotal. My own approach to talking about my sobriety was the same as it had been when I was an active alcoholic: It just wasn't something I talked much about. It wasn't until my first book, where a brief mention of my experience with alcoholism sent a flood of emails to my inbox—many of them from endurance athletes in the sport saying, "Me, too!"—that I realized I was not the only one.

There's no hard data on the overlap of addiction and running, but some anecdotal estimates indicate that as many as 50 percent of adult endurance athletes have a history of substance abuse. Some estimates suggest the number might be even higher in ultrarunning, where extreme personalities tend to find a healthy place to spend the newfound surplus of time and energy that sobriety brings.

Still, it's running's best-kept secret. In a sport populated by people who like to confess, with great sincerity, that their addiction is a single scoop of ice cream after dinner, it rarely seems appropriate to share that we struggle with far worse. So, we simply swap out pretending we're not addicts with pretending that we never were. It's easier that way.

But at Across the Years, people clearly didn't subscribe to that philosophy. Maybe it was because we had so much time, or maybe it was because New Year's is so inextricably linked with partying. Or maybe it was because after running the same 1-mile loop for hours, people are too damn tired to keep up their defenses.

"I started in 2004 after getting off crack," said one runner when I shared I was new to ultrarunning.

"I get that," I said, though I was surprised at such a revelation so early in our conversation. "I'll have six years this August."

"Right on," he said, reaching across to offer a fist bump. "It's gonna be a good year."

Another runner said she got into running through her sponsor at Alcoholics Anonymous. "Trading one high for another," she said with a chuckle. Later on, I met a man who said he had gotten sober because of his dog. Her name was Luna, he said, and she was a boxer. After a particularly long bender, sweet Luna had rested her head on the mattress next to his puffy face and looked at him with sad brown eyes. She hadn't been fed or walked in several days.

"I was so shitty. I let her down. I couldn't do it anymore," he said. "So, I don't use. I can't. I promised her, man." He and Luna started running every day. Even after Luna passed away, the memory of her brown eyes keeps him sober.

I hadn't expected my 24-hour race to turn into a makeshift support group, but there we were, sharing stories, acknowledging the heaviness of an addicted life, and laughing about the dumbass things we used to do. Running for hours (or even days) around a 1-mile loop was also an admittedly dumbass thing to do, we all agreed, but in a different way. A better way.

In recovery, the pendulum often swings from one extreme to the other, and many addicts reinvent themselves as athletes.

Instead of a daily stop at the liquor store on the way home from work, there's a trail run or a track workout that needs to be checked off the training plan. The social outlet one used to find at a bar or club is replaced with the community of endurance athletes. The spiritual hole that used to be in the form of a bottle shape-shifts into a footprint. "Switching one high for another" is certainly an overly tidy cliché, because no matter how poetic it sounds, a runner's high is not the same as a chemically induced one. But it is a high all the same—and a healthier one.

Just before sunset, I finally found Cheryl on the racecourse. Between running at different paces and replenishing our supplies at different times, meeting up, even on a 1-mile loop, proved surprisingly elusive. But we were delighted to spot each other on the course, coming together for another hug.

"I'm on mile 85," said Cheryl. At 61 years old, she occupied a permanent spot on the list of people I wanted to be when I grew up. Her ability to race multiple ultramarathons and triathlons each year was inspiring. "But I'm pretty tired," she said. "How about you?"

"I feel good," I replied. My feet were hurting a little bit, but that was to be expected after nine hours of running. The fun atmosphere of the race and the supportive community of runners made the time fly by. I could hardly believe we had been running for so long. But I couldn't report as to what mile I was on; I had lost track. I also wasn't sure of the last time I had eaten. At various points, I had grabbed bites from the aid station—a boiled potato here, a few crackers there—but I hadn't followed any kind of fueling schedule. I checked my pockets; the gels and bars I had stashed during my last stop at my tent were still there. What time had that been, anyway? "I might be killing off a few brain cells," I joked.

"Welcome to the club, kid," she laughed. "Eat some cookies at the next aid station."

I took her advice, shoveling down a stack of cookies at the start of the next lap. I knew I hadn't been taking in many calories. Although I felt okay, if a bit tired, I decided that I should grab a few pieces of pizza at the next aid station and take a walk break for a lap or two. A warm meal would get me feeling spry again.

But running those 30 minutes to the next aid station was more difficult than I had expected. The sun was going down, and suddenly, so was I. My run pace dwindled to a near-walk. My legs felt heavy, and I stumbled over a section of the course where the path switched from concrete sidewalk to gravel. As I maneuvered to catch my balance, I suddenly felt light-headed.

"You okay?" someone asked. I smiled and gave a quick thumbs-up, moving to the side to let him pass. "Told you to take it easy." It was Grandpa Bill, arms swinging as he power walked past with an I-told-you-so smile on his face.

When the pizza was finally in reach, the smell set off a loud, deep growl in my stomach. With the ferocity of a wild dog, I tore into a slice, grease dripping down my hands and a ring of marinara sauce from nose to chin. I grabbed another slice for the walk ahead. For good measure, I also downed a gel. That would be enough to get back to homeostasis, I reasoned.

I walked another lap, waiting for the food to kick in. And then another lap. The sky melted into an inky black, and the lampposts along the sidewalk flickered on. Volunteers started handing out glow sticks and colorful cellophane leis in anticipation of the midnight party.

I looked at my watch. It was 9:00 p.m. I had been running for 12 hours. On a normal night, I would be getting ready for bed, but this night was far from normal. I was only halfway done with my run, and I wasn't sure how I would make it another 12 hours. What happened to the girl who could stay up all night to ring in the New Year? She would have rallied no matter what.

"Just make it to midnight," I muttered, pumping my arms as I jogged, trying to coax my body into momentum. "It's only three hours. The party will energize you for the rest of the way."

After a few more laps, even that felt too difficult. "Just make it another hour," I negotiated with myself. "If you make it another hour, they're serving ice cream sundaes at the aid station." I had been so focused on forward motion, I hadn't eaten much since those two slices of pizza.

"Just make it another lap. The volunteers will cheer you up." *My feet hurt.*

"Just make it to that damn light post." *It's too dark.*

The last thing I remember of December 31 is thinking that if I changed my socks, maybe my feet would feel fresh and springy again. I don't remember going toward my tent. I don't remember sitting down. I don't remember taking off my shoes.

What I do remember is waking up at 3:00 in the morning on January 1. I squinted and groggily tried to make sense of what was going on.

Where am I? Facedown in the grass next to my tent.

How did I get here? I sat down to change my socks, and . . . maybe I fainted? Not sure.

What time did I go to bed? Based on my watch, sometime after mile 46.

Where the hell are my shoes? I never did find the answer to that question.

Technically, I still had six hours to get back out there and log some more miles. I considered it for a moment and then pushed up on my forearms and crawled into my tent, where I slept until the sun rose for the first time in the new year.

Later that morning, I dove into an aggressive replenishment of glycogen in the form of milkshakes and waffles. As I sat sipping my shake, I listed all the mistakes that had kept me from going the full 24 hours: waking up early and traveling the morning of the race, forgoing the crew, not asking for help, forgetting to eat, not paying attention to warning signs that things were going south, waiting too long to get out of the hole . . . the list went on.

I should have felt upset, and yet I couldn't help but laugh. It figured that the race where I spent hours running with fellow addicts would also be the race where I blacked out. *Of course.* When stuff like this happens, I have to believe that the Endurance Gods are real and that they have a great sense of humor.

You can learn a lot from running. Sometimes, the lessons are powerful and heartening, teaching you that you're capable of so much more than you ever believed. Other times, they're small but poignant—little breakthroughs that add nuance to your understanding of yourself. But the most important lessons are usually delivered in the form of your ass, gift wrapped and handed to you in the most humbling of runs. That's where you really get to the good stuff.

That girl who stayed up all night, drinking champagne and swearing that next year would be better? She doesn't exist anymore. She's been replaced by someone who sips chamomile tea, gets high on endurance, and sometimes even tries to run all night—and fails. But she's not worried about failure or about next year. She's taking things one step and one day at a time. And that's more than enough.

TIRED OR BONKING?
A SIMPLE COMPARISON

For most people, *bonk* is a word associated with a fun activity taking place between the sheets. For runners, however, *bonk* is a word for an experience that is anything but fun. Generally speaking, a *runner's bonk* is defined as "a sudden and precipitous decline in energy levels," but that definition is not entirely accurate. Bonking is more than just feeling tired. You can keep going when you're tired. In a bonk? Not so much. A true bonk is a full-body shutdown, like someone opened a trapdoor on the back of your head and pulled out the AA batteries in your brain.

So how do you tell the difference?

TIRED	VS.	BONKING
You're reading street signs with one eye squinted shut.		You're not reading anything because you have both eyes closed and are praying really, really hard for this race to end. Death would also be acceptable.
You spot a crack in the road, and for a moment, you actually think it's a tiny snake! Oh, wow, that's a good one!		You see a misshapen zombie in a window and scream for a full minute before realizing it is your own reflection. You may never look in a mirror again.
It's taking you an extra few seconds to calculate your average pace and how many miles you have left to go.		Two plus two equals "hahahahaha, [bleep] you, you [bleep]ing [bleep]. Math is [bleep]ing dumb."
Your legs feel a little heavier than normal.		Someone poured actual concrete into your shoes, and you're the only one who can see it.
Cheering spectators on the side of the road are lifting your spirits and keeping you motivated.		If only you could lift your arms, you'd punch every single one of their smiling mouths.
The finish line is so close! Time to dig deep!		Where did those winged goblins come from? And why are they moving the finish line farther away?
You're fantasizing about a post-race pizza.		You want the holy trinity of bonk foods—salt, sugar, and caffeine—and you want it now. Preferably blended together in milkshake form.

UPHILL, BOTH WAYS, IN JORTS

I HADN'T EVEN BEEN IN CUBA for five minutes, and I was already in trouble with the police.

"It's okay," said Mike, our trip leader, squeezing my right shoulder firmly. "Just answer their questions honestly."

"It's okay," said Ana, our other trip leader, as she patted my left arm reassuringly. "Just play dumb, and we'll be out of here in no time."

I wasn't sure whose advice to follow, but in the moment, playing dumb wasn't much of a stretch. I honestly had no clue what was happening. Was it possible I had already committed some kind of cultural gaffe? I replayed the previous five minutes in my head: I stepped off the airplane, walked to the customs gate, and smiled at the agent.

"Passport," he said with a gruff cough. I quickly thrust my little blue booklet forward.

"What is the purpose of your visit?"

"I'm going to Baracoa," I stammered. "For a race."

The customs agent peered over the top of his glasses, assessing whether my face matched the photo in the passport. He shook his head, wrote something on a form, then peered up at me again, double-checking my identity. I smiled nervously, hoping it would detract from the beads of sweat forming on my forehead. He coughed again and pointed at a door: "Go there."

"There" was a holding area next to baggage claim. "There" I found my five travel companions, all of whom had been detained for questioning. It seemed the contents of our suitcases were suspicious to the Cuban authorities, not because they were full of drugs or weapons but because *who the hell travels to Cuba with 10 suitcases full of running shoes?*

The answer: One World Running volunteers. We had arrived in Cuba with more than 200 pairs of shoes in our checked baggage, all of which were to be given to participants of the La Farola run that weekend—that is, if the police would let us. Those 10 suitcases full of running shoes set off all kinds of red flags for the authorities. Were we smuggling in contraband goods?

It was a valid question. For years, trade embargoes have made it difficult for Cuban residents to get US goods. Still, those goods—from iPhones to Nike shoes—are in high demand. I understood that the Cuban government saw US travelers as problematic—particularly, the ones known as *mulas*, or "mules," who smuggle contraband items in their checked luggage for distribution on the Cuban black market. At that moment, our crew of geeky runners sure looked like a bunch of *mulas*.

This is par for the course when traveling with One World Running, a Colorado-based nonprofit organization that provides running shoes to those in need around the world. Every year, volunteers disperse to far-flung corners of the globe, suitcases of shoes in tow, which usually raises a few red flags at the airport, where such cargo is rarely seen. It typically takes a little extra time and coaxing for One World Running volunteers to get through customs—in our case, we were held for four hours, released without our luggage, and told to come back the next day. After a return trip to the airport to plead our case with a supervising officer, we were told we could take our shoes but only after providing a detailed written account of every pair we had brought into Cuba (including brand, color, size, and any distinguishing features). I didn't understand why we had to do it, but I did understand that paperwork was infinitely better than Cuban jail, so *Brooks Running, numero 44, el gris!*

I had arrived in Cuba by way of a story I'd written on Raul Alcolea, a Cuban triathlete with dreams of one day finishing an Ironman race. Nothing could stop him—except the Cuban government. The Caribbean island didn't offer much in the way of triathlon events, yet government officials denied Raul's request to travel outside of the country to participate in an Ironman triathlon. So Raul did what endurance athletes do best: He got stubborn.

On Christmas Eve, 2004, Raul—using a rope to measure the 2.4-mile swim course, a steel bike for a 112-mile ride, and an extremely weathered pair of running shoes for a 26.2-mile run— became a de facto Ironman in Santiago de Cuba. His finish time was 11 hours, 9 minutes, 16 seconds. There was little fanfare at the finish line of his self-made triathlon, but the experience, Raul said, was the best moment of his life.

Trying to connect with Raul for an interview from my office in the United States was a complicated process, as he didn't have a phone number or an email address. Our "interview" involved going through three email contacts and two interpreters, who eventually got a message to Raul in the town of Santiago de Cuba, asking him to make a phone call to another interpreter; my questions were then asked, answered, translated, and emailed back through three contacts to me. Even though I hadn't set foot in Cuba to report the story, I learned that nothing in the country was straightforward.

Still, I loved working on that story. Raul's homemade triathlon was a beautiful contrast to the often overproduced, overwhelming, over-the-top events in America, with thumping dance music at the start line, selfie stations at every mile, and fireworks at the finish. I wasn't sure I possessed the kind of grit Raul exemplified. I like my creature comforts, be they safe courses with police blocking off traffic or the ability to pick from 80 different pairs of shoes at my local running shop. I'm not a fan of making running harder than it needs to be. Hell, I've skipped workouts because it was too windy outside or because I didn't have a clean sports bra to wear. I had never thought of myself as high maintenance, but writing Raul's story made me feel like a Kardashian sister in comparison.

What really got me, though, was a part of the story involving Mike Sandrock, the founder of One World Running. Because triathlon had changed Raul's life for the better, he had started volunteering with Mike and his organization to put running shoes on the feet of Cuba's emerging athletes.

"I remember one time, I came to Cuba with some new gear," Mike said. "After everything was distributed to a group of young runners and triathletes, I took an easy run with Raul. I looked down and saw that he had a worn pair of shoes on that we had given him the year before. 'Raul, where are your new shoes?' I asked. 'I gave them to an athlete who needed them more,' he replied."

Raul's generosity and selflessness took my breath away. People like this actually existed? In Cuba, no less? Like many Americans, my exposure to Cuba had been limited and largely negative—Bay of Pigs, the Cuban Missile Crisis, the bitter diplomatic battle over Elián González—with a strong implication that Cubans were not very good people and that Americans shouldn't interact with them. But Raul's story, along with similar tales Mike shared from his annual service trips to the island, painted a different picture.

Instead of putting together a perspective from other sources, I wanted to decide for myself. Hey, Mike, I wrote in an email after wrapping the story about Raul. Mind if I tag along on your next trip to Cuba?

That would be great, he replied. Do you have a big suitcase? You're going to need it.

One World Running began in 1986 at a marathon in Cameroon, in western Africa. Mike, then a world-class runner who was there racing, was surprised to see that local runners were racing in broken-down plastic sandals—and he was even more surprised that most of them beat him. As a sign of his respect, Mike gave the winner of the race the shoes off his own feet.

When he got home from Cameroon, Mike asked his fellow athletes if they'd be willing to donate used shoes for him to take back to the race the following year. One World Running was not an emotional decision for Mike but rather a highly practical one—runners in Africa needed shoes, and runners in the United States had shoes to spare. It just made sense for him to take a suitcase full of running shoes the next time he traveled.

The emotional side of the organization was discovered the next year in a Boulder, Colorado, laundromat, where Mike was trying—and failing—to wash a load of used, donated shoes. While he was creating a massive mess of tangled shoelaces and spilled detergent, Ana Weir was quietly watching as she folded her own laundry. His incompetence was amusing at first, then pitiful, then infuriating. Did he really not know how a damn washing machine worked? When Mike opened a dryer of shoes only to discover the heat had melted the glue holding the shoes together, Ana couldn't stand it for another second.

"No, no, no!" Ana stepped in, pushing Mike aside. "You're doing it all wrong!" Ana, a Honduran immigrant who worked as a nurse in Boulder, had little patience for floundering. And Mike was floundering in a big way.

"It was a mess," Ana laughs in the warm, animated voice that would become the soundtrack of our Cuba trip. "The man didn't know what he was doing!"

But when Ana heard why Mike was washing a load of used running shoes, she softened. During her childhood in Honduras, not having a pair of shoes meant she couldn't go to school. Eventually, when she became a nurse, she saw firsthand the injuries, parasites, and deformities that came with being barefoot in impoverished areas. And as a runner herself, she knew the bliss that came with a new pair of shoes.

This chance encounter at the laundromat set the tone for a very effective partnership that has lasted several decades: Mike, the one who thinks in problems and solutions, and Ana, the one who actually makes it happen. Since that first pair of shoes in Cameroon, the two have coordinated the distribution of more than 250,000 pairs of new and near-new shoes to runners around the world.

The marquee event for One World Running is the La Farola run, held every year since 2011 in the seaside city of Baracoa, Cuba. Located on the wet and windy side of the Cuchillas del Toa mountains in eastern Cuba, Baracoa is a tough place to get to. In fact, until 1965, the only way to reach the town was by boat. Even today, the lone road over the mountains, named *La Farola* or "lighthouse road," is a tight and treacherous challenge, and it takes half a day to traverse the approximately 150 miles from the airport in Holguín.

It was while running on this road that Mike first met Arnaldo Campos, a local running coach. The two became fast friends, sharing miles and life stories as they climbed the steep ascents of La Farola. At some point in the conversation, Campos revealed that there weren't many organized racing opportunities for runners in Cuba. Even in Baracoa, there was no track—just a dirt path around the crumbling concrete bleachers of what used to be a baseball stadium, where runners clocked their laps in bare feet.

"We can start a race here," Mike replied matter-of-factly. And so he did, returning the following year with Ana, a fistful of donated medals, and two suitcases filled with shoes. The La Farola race, a point-to-point 28-kilometer (17-mile) run up and over the 2,000-foot-tall mountain pass, was the first organized road race in Baracoa. Since that first race, the La Farola run has blossomed, attracting more than 300 elite runners from all over Cuba. Many of these athletes spend days traversing the island on *colectivos*, or shared shuttles in the backs of Soviet-era pickup trucks, which spew thick black smoke as they slowly sputter up and over the mountains of Cuba.

For these runners, the arduous trip to Baracoa is well worth it. After all, there's a race, a medal, and—perhaps most important— a free pair of running shoes.

On our drive to Baracoa, Ana explained that with an average salary of $30 per month, most Cubans lack expendable income for things like running shoes. Their government gives them what they *need*—food, education, and health care—but little more than that. Even a pair of socks is an exorbitant luxury item. Groceries and supplies are heavily rationed, and homes are sparsely furnished. Specialty running stores don't exist. Most people don't have reliable access to cell service or Wi-Fi, much less the ability to look up training plans, register for races, or buy shoes online.

And still, they run. During our three days in Baracoa, I was astounded time and again by the abundance of runners in the most unlikely conditions. On the first day, I met Campos, Mike's friend and cofounder of the La Farola run. He led us on a running tour of Baracoa, from the brightly colored *Parque Central* in old town to the crumbling *malecón* ("esplanade") along the waterfront. In 2016, Hurricane Matthew bulldozed the city, and it never fully recovered. Apartment buildings were missing entire exterior walls, which residents fashioned out of clothesline and fabric or pieces of corrugated metal. As Campos led us away from the city center, the roads turned from concrete to dirt, and the homes from brick to plywood.

Like the Pied Piper, Campos would whistle, and local runners would join the group one by one, looping through neighborhoods and past the crumbling baseball stadium, where Campos led the runners in a track workout around the dirt path.

"This is my favorite place to run," Campos said, gesturing to the clouds of dust kicked up by the runners as they rounded piles of exposed rebar and concrete. He was proud of the joy that running had brought to his community. This, I would come to learn, was a prevailing attitude here: enjoying the simple things.

For the most part, the Cuban people have next to nothing, and there's a constant threat that even that will be taken away. About a year after Hurricane Matthew, Campos had finally replaced the roof on the rickety, wooden one-room structure that housed his family, only to have it torn off again by Hurricane Irma soon after. Like most Cubans, he simply went about rebuilding—first, helping his neighbors; then, repairing his own home. "Also," he noted proudly, "practice was not canceled."

On the day of the La Farola race, the resolve of Cuban runners was even more evident. The race was scheduled to begin at 9:00 a.m., but a few of the buses carrying athletes to the start line had broken down, delaying the start. When the buses finally arrived, the runners filed out in jean shorts, makeshift sports bras crafted from bikini tops, cotton T-shirts, and massive smiles. They ran up and over the mountain passes of La Farola, ducking out of the way of cars on the tight switchbacks of the course, which was not closed to traffic. Instead of water stations, small children dipped the same metal cups, over and over, into a bucket of water procured from a roadside stream. A few farmers set out bushels of fruit on the side of the road for midrace fuel. When runners crossed the finish line, they got a medal and the opportunity to pick out a pair of shoes.

It's often said that spending time in less affluent countries teaches Americans to never take anything for granted. Running in Baracoa forced me to reconsider the luxuries I have on a daily basis: I've never had to run in tattered shoes or make a pair last for a year or more, and I've never been forced to go without footwear altogether. I don't choke on the thick exhaust of Soviet-era vehicles while I'm out for a run. I've never had a problem finding reliable transportation to a race. I don't need to carry a bushel of bananas on a run when there are small foil packages of special squishy gels. I can have those gels, along with just about anything else, Amazon Primed to my house in two days. And my minor hassles of contacting a Cuban triathlete for an interview or getting a suitcase full of shoes through customs suddenly seemed trivial in comparison to the larger, systemic challenges Cubans deal with every day.

But distributing shoes to elated runners at La Farola was much more than simply a realization of privilege. On more than one occasion, an adult finisher would approach the shoe selection table with a younger boy or girl—a family member, a neighbor's kid, or perhaps a young student they taught at the local school—and request a pair of shoes on the child's behalf. They could make their own shoes last another year, they said. It was more important to give the kids the right footwear so that they, too, could enjoy running.

The pleasure of running doesn't come from fancy shoes or medals. When Campos pointed at the dilapidated track and declared it his favorite place, he didn't see the dirt track as lacking in anything. Instead, he saw a place where his community experienced joy and freedom. Ana didn't reach out to Mike in the laundromat because she thought it would lead to a lucrative and whirlwind career helping thousands around the world; she did so because she had the opportunity to help the one person standing in front of her. When Mike gave his own shoes to that runner in Cameroon, the motivation wasn't just practical; it was also a way to connect.

Of the many things I took away from my experience in Cuba, probably the biggest surprise was the realization that we're not so very different after all. I went to Cuba assuming that politics or prejudice would create divisions among us or expose differences too cavernous to cross. Neither was the case. There was no disdain or nationalism to address. I liked them, they liked me, and we all liked running. And even though I may surely seem like a Kardashian by comparison, it turns out I have a lot in common with someone who races barefoot and in jean shorts. Indeed, I left Cuba with an aim to be a bit *more* like people who race barefoot and in jean shorts, as they seemed to have a lot of important things figured out.

On our final night in Baracoa, we shared a meal with Campos and the local team of La Farola race volunteers. As the evening wound down, Mike stood and raised his glass in a toast to another successful race. He spoke in practical terms—of how many runners participated and how many shoes were distributed. For another year, runners had a race and shoes. The event was a success.

Then his countenance softened as he looked out over the mixed group of Cuban and American volunteers gathered around the table.

"It starts with running and builds into deep, lasting friendship," Mike said, his voice breaking a little. "We're all connected. When you run, it doesn't matter who you are or where you're from or even if you speak the same language."

He put his hand over his heart, pressing down and squeezing as if to contain a sudden, unexpected burst of gratitude. "We're all just part of this one world, you know?"

A HELLUVA RACE
IN A HELLUVA TOWN

RIDING AN ELEVATOR TO THE TOP of China's Shanghai Tower, 128 stories high, takes approximately 40 seconds via a technological marvel noted in the *Guinness Book of World Records* as the fastest elevator in the world. But Suzy Walsham of Australia would rather take the stairs—all 3,398 of them. It's not *that* much slower, after all; running the Shanghai Tower took her only 20 minutes and 44 seconds, a performance that contributes to her top standing in the Towerrunning World Association.

Suzy, who entered (and won) her first "vertical marathon" in 2006, has dominated most of the 90 stair races she's entered since then. The sport, which involves sprinting up the stairwells of the world's tallest towers, has helped her become more fit in other forms of racing as well.

"I did 17:05 for 5K and 36:39 for 10K races last year," says the 44-year-old. "Tower running has improved the strength and power in my legs, and I think mentally I am stronger, too, because tower running events are so tough." Running on flat surfaces feels, well, pretty easy after scaling buildings, she says with a grin.

I was interviewing Suzy ahead of the Empire State Building Run-Up, the ultimate uphill race that doesn't feature a single hill. Once a year, the 102-story New York City skyscraper closes to the public at 8:00 p.m. to give 500 runners the chance to climb one of the world's most recognizable buildings.

"Are there any secrets you can tell me about doing the race?" I asked Suzy.

She hesitated for a moment and then laughed. "The first time is special. I wouldn't ruin it for you."

In general, I don't take the stairs. I am strictly an elevator gal. Ask anyone with asthma, and they'll likely tell you the same—even just one flight can set off a bout of coughing and wheezing that can last for hours. This can be pretty embarrassing, especially if you find yourself forced to take the stairs with your colleagues, who note your heavy panting with a puzzled look: "I thought you, like, ran marathons and stuff."

Now take that and multiply it by 86—that was the feat ahead of me at the Empire State Building Run-Up. Eighty-six flights,

1,586 individual stairs, 1,050 vertical feet—no matter how you cut it, the race looked like a whole lotta inhaler puffs.

But, as it turned out, it wasn't the race that took my breath away. I'm used to asthma attacks during races. I'm even used to those attacks starting just before races, when my nerves kick in. But I had never experienced an asthma attack as a direct result of the man of my dreams standing next to me.

(Before I continue, let me apologize to my husband. I swear, darling, you run a very close second.)

It happened in the lobby of the Empire State Building, five minutes before I was to run up all those stairs to the observation deck on top. Standing next to me was Patrick Wilson, star of Broadway, movies, and 99 percent of my sexual fantasies. (You know what, honey? Maybe just skip ahead to the next chapter.)

I didn't know it was him at first. At the time, my mind was solely on the nerve-wracking feat that lay just ahead of me. My wave was one of the first to go, following the elite racers (which included Walsham, who went on to take her ninth consecutive victory in an astonishing 12 minutes and 56 seconds). I had been assigned to the "media" wave, made up mostly of indignant sports journalists whose managers thought sending a former linebacker named "Champ" to the race would make a good puff piece on the 11 o'clock news. As we milled about the start line, watching the countdown clock tick back from five minutes, another sports bro squeezed into the empty space next to me.

"Hey," he said.

"Hey," I nodded in acknowledgment. And then I saw those eyes, and all at once my brain flooded: *Holy shit, this isn't a sports bro. This is Patrick Wilson.*

"How's it going?" he said with a smile.

I stared. "Fine," I gawked. *Holy shit, Patrick Wilson is smiling at me. Holy shit, holy shit, holy shit, holyshitholyshitholyshit.*

As it turned out, the "media" wave was actually the "media and celebrity" wave. I don't know why they would put those two populations together, because in general, media folks tend to be some of the most awkward individuals on the planet. Exhibit A: me, trying to play it cool as I patted my hip pocket to locate my inhaler, because *Patrick Wilson is smiling at me, and I can't breathe.*

I tried to say, "It's going great!" but all that came out was a cough, followed by a few quick gasps for breath.

"You okay?" he asked. *Patrick Wilson wants to know if I'm okay. Patrick Wilson cares about me. Patrick Wilson is in love with me. BE COOL, DAMMIT.*

I snapped out of my gawk, blinking my eyes rapidly. "Yeah, I'm good. How are you?"

He smiled again and gave me the most adorable thumbs-up. I tried to keep from melting into a puddle on the floor. An awkward silence followed as the clock ticked down: three minutes to start.

"Have you done this race before?" he asked.

"No. Have you?"

"Yes. I'm trying to beat my time from last year."

More awkward silence. Patrick Wilson looked away for a moment, and I seized the opportunity to take a hit off my asthma inhaler, hoping he wouldn't notice. But instead of making the quick *poof* sound it was supposed to, the apparatus whistled loudly as I took the medicine into my lungs, causing the man of my dreams to turn back in my direction.

"You sure you're okay?"

"Totally," I squeaked. *Why is my voice so high pitched? I SAID, BE COOL, DAMMIT.*

With two minutes to go, Patrick Wilson offered up the lessons he learned last year: ease into it, take the stairs two at a time, and use the handrail to pull yourself up. I managed to stutter out a joke that my only goal for the race was to not die.

"You're going to do great," he said, giving me a pat on the back. *Patrick Wilson touched me because he is in love with me. BE COOL. Also, INHALE, YOU DUMBASS.*

I stifled an asthmatic cough and wondered what would happen if I passed out right there. Would Patrick Wilson perform CPR on me? I ran my tongue along my teeth, trying to determine if I had the adequate hygiene for sucking face with Patrick Wilson. Had I brushed my teeth after dinner? I couldn't remember. I wished they made a mint-flavored asthma inhaler for occasions like these.

"Ten, nine, . . . ," the announcer boomed.

"Good luck," Patrick Wilson smiled. I didn't even notice when the air horn blew, marking the start of the race. I was too busy naming our future children and/or rescue dogs.

RUN, YOU DUMBASS. I took off through the black-and-gold art deco lobby of the Empire State Building, following the directions of the guards in their iconic burgundy suits.

I knew running up 86 flights of stairs would be a unique challenge in and of itself. Unlike the ski jump of the Red Bull 400, which featured a 35-degree incline, the stairs of the Empire State Building were an even steeper 65 degrees. (For comparison, Filbert Street, one of San Francisco's steepest roads, is a mere 17.5 degrees, and the Boston Marathon's legendary Heartbreak Hill is a paltry 4.5 degrees.) But what I didn't know was that the environment added another layer of difficulty. For some reason, I had assumed the stairwell would be just as opulent as the Empire State Building, with tiled floors, gold-plated rails, and climate control. And that was the case for the first two floors, until a burgundy suit opened a fire exit and motioned for me to enter.

No one warned me that the stairwell of the Empire State Building is opened only a few times a year. Once in a while, the New York City Fire Department cracks the doors for a fire drill; otherwise, the race is the only time the stairs see any action. As a result, it's hot, stuffy, and dusty. By the 10th story, my mouth was dry. By the 20th, I had shifted from a jog up the stairs to more of a lunge, taking the stairs two at a time.

Because the race is in the fire exit stairwell, there are no spectators, save for a burgundy-clad guard every five flights who makes the same joke: "Should've taken the elevator. It's faster." If you wanted to bail out on these floors, you got the sense the guards wouldn't let that happen. *You made your idiot bed, now lie in it.*

By the 40th floor, I had lost count of where I was. By the 50th, a familiar taste coated my tongue. *Metal,* I thought. *I'm dying again.* By the 65th, my legs were pillars of lime gelatin.

"Should've taken the elevator," a burgundy suit chortled once again. "It's faster." But before I had a chance to give him my best sarcastic chortle, a door swung open, hitting me with a *whoosh* of cold, invigorating fresh air.

That's another thing no one had told me about the Empire State Building Run-Up: Before you cross the finish line, the course follows a victory lap around the observation deck. Though I was in a race against the clock (and 499 other runners), I deliberately slowed to take it all in. I had never been to the top of the Empire State Building before, much less at nighttime, when I could see the vast expanse of New York City twinkling below in all her big-city glitz and glamour.

It was a cold February night, and the wind swirled around me as steam radiated off my body. For the first time that evening, I stopped to take a deep breath. *Is this really happening?* I laughed as I jogged toward the finish line. This was all just too cool.

"Hey! You didn't die!" Patrick Wilson was sitting on the floor just past the finish line, still panting from his own race as he waved me in for a high five. Even with a bright red face and a shirt soaked with sweat, he was still hella dreamy.

For 20 minutes of my time (and two days of post-race muscle soreness), I received a nifty art deco medal saying I had finished the Empire State Building Run-Up. But that wasn't the reward—that came far before the finish line.

As runners, we tend to think in exchanges and zero sum games: If I finish this race, I get a medal. If I run 10 miles today, I'll have earned this burger. I have to hit these splits, otherwise, I failed. But sometimes, the things we get out of a run are far more abstract than a piece of tin to wear around our neck or a set of numbers on a stopwatch. A run can take us to places and people we would otherwise never have the opportunity to encounter.

Truth be told, I lost my Empire State medal shortly after finishing the race. I think I forgot to pack it in my luggage when I left New York City. But that's okay—anytime someone mentions New York City, I'm quick to share that time I ran to the top of the Empire State Building. It's always a hit; my "Free Bird" at parties and meetings, if you will. I pull that anecdote out far more often than I would a race medal. Also, I finally have a good retort for when my colleagues give me grief for getting winded on the stairs.

And every time I pull out my asthma inhaler, I get the best reward of all: a fleeting reminder of my hot, breathless encounter* in an Empire State Building stairwell with that dreamboat, Patrick Wilson.

*That's my story, and I'm sticking to it.†
† Sorry, honey.

GRANDPA'S
IN THE TUFF SHED

IT'S POSSIBLE THAT THIS TOME in your hand will be the last book I ever write. Not because I'm retiring from writing or because books are a so-called dying art in current society's Candy Crush world. No, my publishing fate may have been sealed the day I handed each of my bosses a blue full-body spandex suit and asked as gently as I could: "Would you mind putting this on?"

And then, in hopes of lessening the blow: "We have tutus, if you're feeling modest."

It was a desperate, last-minute request. Two of our team members had dropped out of the Frozen Dead Guy Days annual

Coffin Race, and we needed bodies—badly. The rules of the race explicitly state that all teams must have seven people—six runners plus one corpse.

"Corpse?" Casey choked on the word when I asked if she'd be willing to be our dead person.

"Yeah . . . ," I struggled for something convincing to say. "Hey, what's great is, we all have to run, but you get to just lie there . . . uhm, in a coffin."

My voice trailed off. Yeah, this was going to be a tough sell.

Every March, the tiny town of Nederland, Colorado, fetes its most famous resident: Bredo Morstoel, locally known as Colorado's Coolest Grandpa. If you want to visit Grandpa Bredo, just follow the winding roads to Barker Reservoir and look for the gray Tuff Shed with red trim. But be warned: Grandpa Bredo isn't particularly chatty. That's because Grandpa Bredo is dead. He has been since 1989, though he looks surprisingly fresh for a dead dude. Dry ice will do that for a guy.

The story of Bredo Morstoel is as surreal as it gets. After Bredo died of a heart attack in Norway, his grandson, Trygve Bauge, transported his body to the United States to be cryogenically suspended. Trygve believed that even though Grandpa had already kicked the bucket, freezing the body would allow Trygve to one day bring Grandpa back from the dead, when he could then—well, I'm not sure—resume doing 1989 Grandpa things, I presume, such as playing Chinese checkers and offering up the stale butterscotch candies that have been in his pocket for the past 30 years. Look, the guy transported a dead body thousands of miles with the intention of reanimating him in 200 years. Is any rationale going to sound reasonable?

But I digress. Back to Grandpa. Upon arriving in the United States, Bredo was stored in liquid nitrogen at a California cryonics facility. But cryogenic storage is costly, and in 1993, Trygve, in a move that would make the most interesting / most disturbing home-improvement show ever, decided to take the do-it-yourself route. He built a small shed behind his home in Nederland, stocked it full of dry ice, and moved Grandpa Bredo into the cooler.

Everyone was doing dandy until 1995, when authorities discovered that Trygve had overstayed his visa. Oh, and also? He was keeping a dead guy out back. It's unclear which offense triggered Trygve's deportation, but he was on a one-way flight to Norway faster than you can say, "WTF?"

The town of Nederland was left holding the Bredo bag. Although Trygve had stocked the shed with dry ice just prior to his deportation, time was ticking down, and Bredo would soon thaw out. Residents were unhappy, and rightfully so; the once-quiet town had become a three-ring circus. News vans and purveyors of the morbid were blocking streets and extrapolating Trygve's own peculiarities to all residents: Nederland was clearly into some freaky shit.

Nederland could have let Bredo defrost. They could have given him a proper burial, or even a Norwegian Viking funeral on the waters of the Barker Reservoir. But when it came time to vote on the next step, a small group of Trygve's neighbors stepped forward and offered to maintain the Tuff Shed. They liked Trygve, after all. Aside from the whole dead grandpa thing, he had always been a pretty good neighbor.

Ever since that fateful day in 1995, Grandpa Bredo has been resting in peace on dry ice, 1,800 pounds of which are delivered to the shed every month by Nederland residents. (Though the city decided to let Bredo stay, they did add a clause to the municipal code against the keeping of dead bodies. They made an exemption for Grandpa Bredo under—rim shot, please—a grandfather clause. *Hey-ooooo!*)

The three-ring circus never really died down after Bredo was discovered. No matter how much they tried to minimize the whole fiasco, Nederland couldn't shake its reputation of "that town where freaky shit happens." So, in 2002, they decided to double down on their reputation: *You want to see freaky shit? We'll give you freaky shit.* They created the Frozen Dead Guy Days festival, and Nederland was never the same.

The weekend-long festival is a bazaar of bizarre, with Grandpa Bredo as the mascot. In addition to free visits to the Tuff Shed, the weekend includes ice carving, a polar plunge, frozen turkey bowling, a slushie-drinking contest, frozen facial hair competition, and lots of people dressed as frozen zombies. Also, this being Colorado, there's a lot of weed to facilitate the freakiness.

A highlight of the weekend is the Coffin Race. Spectators pack the stands of a makeshift outdoor arena to watch costumed teams race with a "corpse" in a handcrafted coffin through a course full of mud, snow, water, and obstacles. Although the races are structured in a double-elimination style, there are three winners: best time, best theme, and most notable snafu.

Our team wanted to win them all. As a collection of endurance athletes, we approached coffin racing with the same dedication as we would a marathon or triathlon. Neil brought his engineering know-how to calculate the best trajectories in and through the obstacles. Sig, a doctor, secured the use of a lightweight metal stretcher normally used for backcountry rescues to craft our coffin. Bekki, with her eye for design, scoured thrift shops and costume stores for unique and creative elements to add to our bright blue, full-body spandex suits, known as *zentai*. Jason brought the vodka. The only talent I had was the maturity level of a 13-year-old boy, so I came up with our team name: The Blue Balls.

We had two other team members, who will go unnamed because they failed us. One was injured and said she probably shouldn't run. The other had gotten into Jason's vodka and *definitely* couldn't run. It was race morning, and we were screwed. The rules state you cannot enter the race without a full team of seven. We had a serious problem.

"What if we just asked some people at the festival to be on our team?" Bekki asked.

"And place our fates in the hands of strangers?" Sig barked. "Silence. Don't talk unless you have a winning idea." He would accept nothing less than victory at the Coffin Race.

"Well, we don't know anyone who lives around here, so it seems we're out of luck then," she said, shrugging.

I felt Neil looking at me from across the kitchen table. I didn't want to meet his eye; I knew exactly what he was thinking. I finally returned his gaze with a subtle shake of the head, sending a clear message through spousal telepathy: *No, we're not doing it.* Neil raised his eyebrows: *But we could ask them.* I glared and shook my head again: *Not a chance.* Neil cleared his throat.

"So, Susan actually knows some people who live down the hill . . . "

By the time Neil finished explaining that my bosses lived in the nearby city of Boulder, my teammates were thrusting a cell phone into my hands, demanding that I text them immediately. I had no choice.

Prior to arriving in Nederland, Neil and I had spent a night in Boulder. It's where my publishing house is located, and since I was going to be in the neighborhood anyway, I scheduled some meetings and promotional interviews for my first book. It was a chance for me to say hello in person—a rarity in the publishing world, where all work is conducted, understandably, in writing. Emails are so standard, in fact, that I had collaborated with the publishing staff on an entire book before they ever learned I was deaf. It had never come up in our daily email conversations. It wasn't until my publicist started talking about scheduling podcast interviews that I realized I had some explaining to do. It was an eye-opening experience—the realization that you can talk to someone every single day and yet not really know them at all.

It was great to spend time with the team at the publishing house. I loved the chance to discuss the success of and lessons learned from my first book, while also brainstorming ideas for my next one. I left the meeting feeling confident that I would enjoy a long, happy relationship with my publisher, Renee, and editor, Casey. They seemed to truly value my ideas and were just as great in person as they had been in emails. Organized, resolute, and professional, they were the perfect handlers for someone like me, who was none of those things. I had many books I wanted to write for them, and they sounded excited about the possibilities.

And now my teammates were asking me to put all of that in jeopardy by asking these two dignified professionals—my bosses, for heaven's sake—to be part of a coffin race. Wearing full-body spandex. On a team named "The Blue Balls."

Swallowing hard, I typed the text message reluctantly: Are you guys still planning on coming up today?

They had mentioned the day before that they hoped to come up to the festival for an hour or two to catch the coffin race and cheer us on.

We're on our way now! came Casey's cheery reply.

I paused. Then texted, Any chance you'd want to be in the race? We're two people short . . .

I held my breath as I hit "Send." Bekki, Sig, and Neil leaned in, staring at my phone with anticipation. A few interminable minutes passed. Then a few more. Finally, the phone buzzed, breaking the stillness of the room. I held the phone far away from my face and peered through squinted eyes, as if opening the message was akin to detonating a bomb on my writing career.

Sure! Count us in, was the reply.

Twenty minutes later, I was handing them their zentais and apologizing profusely for the what-the-fuckery that was about to take place.

"Please don't fire me," I pleaded.

"It will be fun," Renee said cheerfully, as she sifted through our costume box, holding up the variety of options Bekki had accumulated for people to accessorize their spandex: helmet with Viking horns, shaggy 1970s fur coat, headbands festooned with glittery blue disco balls. When Renee held up a pair of bedazzled men's briefs with a raised eyebrow, I was certain she was wondering if she had spoken too soon.

As a prerequisite for coffin racing, all teams had to first participate in the Frozen Dead Guy Days parade, a slow crawl through the streets of Nederland. When we arrived, the parade staging area was bustling with oddity: lumberjacks in flannel and boots, a Beetlejuice-themed team in black-and-white stripes, the cast of *Sesame Street*, a unit of unicorns toting a rainbow-clad coffin, a group of Egyptians carrying King Tut, zombies in gold lamé outfits declaring DISCO IS DEAD. And then there was us—The Blue Balls, in shiny spandex covering our bodies and faces (thank goodness), carrying a coffin that clinked with every step thanks to the cobalt testicles dangling from the stretcher.

"I love a parade!" Casey said, marveling at the lineup of colorful coffin teams as she climbed into the coffin and lay down.

"Me, too!" Bekki tittered. "It's like we're in the Olympics!"

Renee and I looked at each other and exploded in laughter. It was all so ridiculous.

"If we're going to do this," Renee insisted, "we've got to go for the gold."

Sig gave a nod of approval, his Viking horns bobbing in the air. "I like you," he said, giving Renee a playful slug on the shoulder. "You're a champion. I can tell."

Renee was right: If we were going to be weird, we were going to be weird all the way. At various points in the parade, as we waltzed through the streets of Nederland, one of us would yell a command and the team would all follow suit, waving like beauty queens, dropping our Casey-corpse, running Chinese fire drills around the coffin, rushing in unison to jump inside a row of porta-potties next to the road. The crowd ate us up. We may have been first-timers to this dance, but baby, we were on fire.

Bolstered by a new confidence, we could hardly wait for the main event. We were definitely feeling cocky. As teams began to line up for the Coffin Race, Neil and Sig scrutinized each team, trying to find their weakest link. They pointed out teams wearing costumes that would hinder fast running, declaring that The

Blue Balls could absolutely beat them because we, as endurance athletes, knew the aerodynamic advantages of spandex. They identified structural issues in coffins that we could ram into should sabotage be required. In the middle of this strategy session, Casey leaned in and tapped Sig on the shoulder.

"If we race those guys," she said in a hushed voice, pointing at a team of jolly-looking pink flamingos, "I know how to get under their skin."

"How?" he asked.

"I'll just go like this," Casey said, running a finger across her blue-spandexed throat in a knife-slashing motion.

Sig nodded. "Ruthless. Wow, I like you, too."

He turned to me. "Susan, why did you wait so long to get them on our team?"

I laughed in disbelief. Was I the only one who thought it was a big deal to ask so much of the people who signed my paycheck?

In our heat, we were slated to race against The Lumberjacks, a virile-looking crew of strapping, flannel-clad students from the nearby university. After staging our coffin at the start line, we huddled for one last strategy session. Neil reviewed the course, which started with a weave through hay bales, went over a mound of snow, and then rounded a corner to a drill station. There, the corpse needed to jump out of the coffin, run to a marked spot, make a snowball, and throw it at a target. Once the target was successfully hit, the corpse would then return to the coffin, and the team would continue on, coffin in tow, through a mud pit and over several more piles of snow before arriving at the finish line.

"We're going to approach the first obstacle from the right." Neil drew a line in the mud like a football coach to illustrate his point. "We want to get out of the gate as fast as possible. If the other team comes near us, we lurch and try to throw them off-balance. From there, it's all about sure feet on the snow. Get your footing."

"And don't fuck it up," Sig added helpfully. "Clear eyes. Full hearts. Blue Balls. Can't lose. Now everyone put your hands in. Blue Balls on three. One, two, three . . ."

"BLUE BALLS!" we hooted, sending the crowd into a loud, raucous cheer. Casey climbed into the coffin with a last plea— "Don't drop me!"

The rest of us crouched beside it in starting position. A countdown ensued, and we took off with the air horn.

We reached the hay bales at precisely the same time as The Lumberjacks, both teams grunting as we strained to push our own coffin through the obstacle first. We won the first battle, sprinting over the mound of snow and rounding the corner. Suddenly the terrain turned slippery, and I lost my footing, executing an indecorous face-plant into the mud as my team sprinted on ahead without me. Desperate to rejoin the team, I slid around in the mud like a baby deer, trying to get upright. But just as I reached a standing position, I was hit from behind— The Lumberjacks.

"No!" I screamed, trying to push through the tangle of flannel above me. But in the same instant, I realized I had an opportunity. There were no rules about sabotage—in fact, it was encouraged.

"Go!" I yelled to my team. "Save yourselves!" I began throwing arms and legs like a drunken octopus, trying to make it harder for The Lumberjacks to get their footing in the mud. Only when I saw Casey's snowball hit the target at the drill station did I let up, sliding out from the melee and sprinting to join my team.

The good news is that we sprinted to the finish line well ahead of The Lumberjacks. Just as Bekki had said, it was exactly like the Olympics—if the Olympics had a crowd screaming "Blue Balls! Blue Balls!" in support of the winning team.

The bad news is that 13 teams overall were faster than us. As it turned out, coffin racing is cutthroat. Some teams practice all year for the event. Although we had won our heat, we hadn't met the qualifying standard for the next round. We also lost in the theme and snafu competitions, a trifecta of disappointment that haunts Sig to this day.

"Well, looks like it's margarita time," Renee said encouragingly, when we saw our placing on the tournament board. "My treat."

We circled up by a big, warm bonfire, laughing, sipping on margaritas and hot chocolates, while reliving the excitement of the race. Neil said he may or may not have head-butted a lumberjack during our standoff at the first obstacle. Sig commended Casey's outstanding snowball-throwing aim. We all laughed about the moment we realized we had a team member down and how worry had turned to glee as said team member thrashed muddily about in sabotage of the other team.

But my favorite part about sitting by the bonfire was looking at Casey and Renee, clad in ridiculous blue spandex, and laughing with my friends. I had been petrified to ask them—my work colleagues—to join this crazy lark, and yet they ended up as our MVPs.

It also surprised me how much fun they were. And I swear I'm not just writing that because my editor and publisher will read this. In their context as my bosses, both are extremely professional. Renee has a keen strategic mind and a clear vision of what she wants from her authors. Casey is a hell of an editor, extracting themes from my manuscripts I sometimes don't even realize are there. But, as it turns out, they are also joyful, adventurous souls. I knew that Casey was an ultrarunner, but only at the bonfire did I learn that she traveled the world doing—and sometimes even winning—difficult multistage races. Renee could right any errant ship at work (and God knows I steer off course on a regular basis), but that day I learned that this was a trait she had honed as someone who fostered and adopted kids with extremely challenging backgrounds. I had emailed them almost daily for the past three years, and yet I realized I really had known nothing about them until today.

Modern technology is, in many ways, the Great Connector. So many conversations take place solely via keyboard or touch screen. Indeed, people have become hesitant to answer the phone, preferring the comfort zone of keystrokes and emojis. But think about the last five people you emailed or texted. Can you recall what their voices sound like? Have you even *heard* what their voices sound like? Perhaps not. And that's probably not the only thing missing in your mental picture. What else don't you know about the person behind that email address? Maybe the person you've been emailing every day is deaf and you had no idea, or maybe they have a fascinating backstory that will leave you openmouthed and speechless with admiration. Or maybe they have a grandpa on dry ice in their backyard. It happened to Trygve, you know.

We think we're connecting, but are we really? Sometimes it takes something crazy to force us to look up from our screens and look at each other, even if it's just to laugh at the absurdity of it all. Had it not been for Grandpa Bredo, I don't know that I ever would have interacted with my bosses outside the context of our work together. I would have stayed in my safe assumptions extracted from our surface-level email exchanges, and that would have been a shame.

To remind me of this, I printed out an action photo from the coffin race and tacked it to the bulletin board above my desk. It makes me laugh every time I look at it. In the center of the photo, Casey is sitting in the coffin, her mouth agape in a happy scream as she grips the sides of her coffin for dear life. She's surrounded by the rest of The Blue Balls, mid-stride in their full-coverage spandex suits. Neil is wearing a Viking helmet, Sig has added blue athletic socks, Renee has a tiny blue tutu, everyone is smiling. In the background, the crowd of spectators is laughing and cheering.

I'm not in the photo. I'm somewhere out of the frame, fighting off Lumberjacks on behalf of my friends, old and new. For the rest of our lives, we'll always have a connection, built off the one-of-a-kind camaraderie that comes with uniting as a team in support of a goal. Oh, and wearing blue spandex suits.

It's like the Olympics. It's *totally* like the Olympics.

THAT'S A HORRIBLE IDEA. WHAT TIME?

I LOOKED TO MY LEFT, where Heidi was standing, her eyes wide and unblinking as she read the sign again and again.

GOING DOWN IS OPTIONAL. COMING UP IS MANDATORY.

Below the sign's block letters were grim statistics from the previous year: 290 search-and-rescue operations, 129 medical helicopter evacuations, 12 deaths.

"You still want to do this?" I asked, nudging her in the rib cage with my elbow to startle her out of her bewilderment.

Heidi took another moment to scan the sign. Slowly, her gaping mouth closed into a smirk.

"Oh, yeah."

Heidi and I have long joked that the majority of our conversations are some variation of the same two statements: "That's a horrible idea. What time?" But it isn't really a joke. For years, we've built a friendship on a solid foundation of questionable decision-making and excellent stories.

Like me, Heidi is an endurance athlete. We met on Twitter, in the days when Twitter was mostly just a place where people posted pictures of their cats. For runners and triathletes, however, Twitter was like a massive, faceless cheering squad: Post something about crushing a hill workout or setting a PR at a race, and hundreds (if not thousands) of fellow endurance athletes would shake their virtual pom-poms.

Except Heidi. Heidi wasn't the cheerleader type. She was more like a whip-cracker, in a good way. When other people offered platitudes, she pushed buttons. If someone spoke in hypotheticals, she told them to stop thinking and start doing. Goading was Heidi's love language:

That's great! What's next?

I bet you could have gone two minutes faster.

Why sign up for the half when you can obviously handle the full?

We lived a thousand miles apart, yet Heidi quickly became one of my favorite virtual training buddies. Whenever I posted something on Twitter about training or racing, I could count on her to say just the right thing, be it inspiration, motivation, or a swift kick in the ass. She always knew what I needed to hear, even when I didn't know what I needed to hear.

When I was assigned to cover an Ironman race in Texas, where she lived, we achieved our first milestone of questionable decision-making: meeting someone from the internet. Heidi was going to be volunteering at the swim exit, while I was there to snap photos and report on the event.

It turned out that she was just as sassy in person as she was online, yelling at athletes to stop walking in their transition from the swim leg to the bike portion of the race and start running: "Every second counts, y'all!" she bellowed, clapping her hands to accentuate each syllable. When one swimmer stumbled onto shore, panting heavily, Heidi got down on her hands and knees and helped him remove his wetsuit.

"That . . . was . . . really . . . hard," he gasped.

"Of course it's hard. It's Ironman," Heidi said kindly but firmly. She handed him his wetsuit and pointed toward the bike course. "Better get going."

I liked her on Twitter, but I loved her in person. Heidi was no nonsense, no excuses, and no bullshit. We were constantly pushing each other to do more and be better. At that first meeting in Texas, Heidi confided that she had been thinking about signing up for an Ironman race herself; I promised her that if she did, I'd fly out to cheer her on. When I said something about the insanity of a "Birthday Swim," the endurance athlete's term for swimming 100 laps of 100 meters each, Heidi's response was

"Let's do it next week." We agreed on a time and then texted each other before diving into the pool in our separate states. Post-swim, we texted photos of our GPS watches (smack talk may or may not have accompanied said photos).

This driving force spilled over into other areas of our lives as we encouraged each other to dream big dreams and take big risks, like enrolling in graduate school (Heidi) or spending way too much money for front-row tickets for a Backstreet Boys concert (not Heidi—but also, totally worth it). In other words: *That's a horrible idea. What time?*

So, when I decided I would run the Grand Canyon on my 35th birthday, I knew exactly whom I wanted to invite.

I called her up and dove right in: "Hey, would it be crazy if—"

"Yes," Heidi interrupted. "So, what are we doing?"

I laid out my plan: Less than 1 percent of people who go to the Grand Canyon each year make it to the bottom, where the Colorado River twists and turns through the massive rock formations of its own creation. I wanted to know what it looked like down there. I wanted to do something epic for my birthday. I wanted to be a 1-percenter. I wanted to run across the Grand Canyon.

Heidi didn't hesitate: "That's a horrible idea. I'll book my flight right now."

For many runners, running the Grand Canyon is a bucket-list item, nestled somewhere between the Badwater 135 ultra-marathon and the Boston Marathon. But unlike most bucket-list races, the Grand Canyon doesn't require the runner to pay an entry fee or meet a qualifying standard. You just have to be plucky enough to show up and think you can do it.

And this confidence will be tested many times, even before running across the Canyon. A Google search of "running the Grand Canyon" yields dozens, if not hundreds, of results that all say it's a terrifically bad idea. For starters, it's a pretty big hole to traverse: 24 miles across and 6,000 feet deep. The trail, which follows a natural break in the canyon rim, is steep and unstable in parts. Runners have to manage the thin air of altitude at the upper levels and intense heat at the lower levels. There are long stretches with no potable water, requiring runners to carry their own and ration wisely. A bonk or injury in the Grand Canyon can't be fixed by hitching a ride or using a cell phone to call for help. Anyone who goes down is expected to come back up under his or her own power.

Training for the thing also presents a challenge. It's such a unique environment that it's hard to replicate the "upside down mountain," as it's known in running circles. Besides, physical fitness is only part of the equation of a successful Grand Canyon run. Upon Heidi and I arriving at the park the night before our big run, a ranger told us about 24-year-old Margaret Bradley, who had died of dehydration while attempting to run across the canyon in 2004. Bradley had finished 31st among women in the Boston Marathon earlier that year, so she certainly had the fitness to do the run. But insufficient water and fuel, coupled with hot temperatures at the bottom (the temperature in the shade that day was 105 degrees Fahrenheit), led to her untimely death.

And that wasn't all. The ranger proceeded to recite a whole litany of perils runners could encounter on the trails: falls, shifting sands, scorpions, rattlesnakes, excrement from the pack mules that shuttle supplies to the campsite at the bottom of the canyon.

"Donkey poop is dangerous?" I raised a skeptical eyebrow.

"If you're not paying attention when you step in it, it can be very slippery."

I searched for a sign of sarcasm. There was none. Donkey shit was a legit concern.

Signs all over the park warned of the perils of venturing past the rim of the canyon. The more we learned of the risk, the more I started to second-guess our plan. The night before our run, while bundled up in a campsite just off the trailhead, I had vivid and terrifying dreams of falling into the canyon. Each time, I'd startle awake moments before hitting the waters of the Colorado River. Just as I finally fell into something resembling sleep, Heidi poked me awake. It was 5:00 a.m. Go time.

We loaded our running packs with water and supplies, our worries seesawing between having too much and not having enough. How could we know what we would need for a day like this?

"Do you think we've forgotten anything?" I asked as I worked to zip up a bulging pocket of my pack.

Heidi let out a soft grunt as she slung a full water bladder over her shoulder. "I suppose we'll find out in the hole. Let's go."

We left the campsite just as dawn began to paint the sky with soft pastels. In the 30-degree, crisp morning air, every exhaled breath wafted out in soft white tendrils. At the start of the trail, we encountered the bold-lettered sign warning of the risk of crossing the trailhead: **GOING DOWN IS OPTIONAL. COMING UP IS MANDATORY.**

"You still want to do this?"

"Oh, yeah."

It was official: We were going on an adventure. Together, we descended the tight, rocky switchbacks of the trail, each step taking us farther away from civilization. Our cell phones lost reception. We were entirely on our own, but it wasn't scary—it was exciting. Heidi lifted her arms and started singing "Into the Great Wide Open" at the top of her lungs. Her pure joy—not to mention her passionate attempt at Tom Petty's nasally singing— made me laugh out loud.

"Sing with me!" Heidi insisted. "No one can hear us!"

We laughed and sang as we descended deeper and deeper into the canyon, eventually losing sight of the rim. As we turned a corner, Heidi stopped suddenly and grabbed my arm.

"Look!" she said with a gasp. Below us was a maze of red-rock mesas, bisected by a bright blue ribbon: the Colorado River. By now, the sun had crested over the top of the canyon walls, unveiling the landscape in all its splendor.

We hadn't set out into the Grand Canyon with any time goal in mind. The challenge was so unique, we had no way of predicting how long it would take us to finish. In our everyday world, running just under a marathon distance was something we could complete start to finish and still make our brunch reservation. But with the extreme heat and 12,000 feet to get down one side and up the other, we had no idea how long we'd be out here. As we perched on the overlook and took in the view, one thing was clear: This wasn't a race. Heidi and I were going to take our sweet time and enjoy this exceptional view. We pulled off our packs and gawked.

Suddenly Heidi broke the silence.

"Happy birthday!" She leaned over and pulled a small foil package out of her pack. "I got you something."

She had brought birthday cake–flavored gels just for the occasion. We opened two packs, toasted, and slurped them down in one go. It was the best birthday breakfast I could have asked for.

The sun was getting higher in the sky, temperatures were rising, and it was time to move on. About a mile from the river, we encountered our first humans of the day: a foursome of hikers with silver hair and army-green vests. As we passed them, we said hello and slowed to chat. One of the hikers, a slim woman with knobby knees and a wide smile, raised her hiking poles and cheered us on.

"It's so great to see the young ladies out here doing this!" she exclaimed.

"Oh, we're not exactly young," I laughed.

"I wouldn't say we're ladies, either," Heidi added.

As it turned out, our new friends were celebrating a birthday in the Canyon, too. Tom, a broad-shouldered man with a thick white mustache, turned 70 years old that day. After we exchanged wishes for a safe climb out of the canyon and continued on our path, Heidi looked back over her shoulder at the group and smiled.

"I guess we know how we're celebrating your birthday in another 35 years." She'd read my mind.

When we reached the bottom of the canyon, it was already a toasty 90 degrees. We threw off our packs and waded into the river, soaking our legs in the bracing, crystal-clear water. Snacking on sandwiches we had prepped the night before, we let the cool, gentle current massage our tired legs in preparation for the formidable climb ahead. Aside from a few hikers downstream, we had the shoreline to ourselves.

"I can't believe people go their entire lives without doing this," said Heidi. She was right. We were breathing in rare air, and we knew it. It felt fantastic. I had been to the Grand Canyon before, but visits had involved squeezing myself into crowded overlooks to get a glimpse of one of the natural wonders of the world. I had perched at the rim, peering down into the layers of pink and brown rock, trying to comprehend its transformation as the river had carved deeper into the stone over millions of years.

As I gazed up at a perfect blue sky, knee-deep in cool water, I thought about those earlier trips. Back then, it had never occurred to me to actually go to the bottom and experience it for myself. Before I took up running, the idea of covering 24 miles, much less up and down precariously steep canyon trails, seemed impossible. Even once I had started running, it didn't sound much easier. Running the Grand Canyon was something someone else might do, but definitely not me. I had never considered myself the type of athlete who was strong enough to take on such a challenge. That was for the super-fit—the real runners. And yet, there I was, at the bottom of a canyon so vast and so deep I couldn't see the top rim. I had a perspective of the canyon that few people would ever see. And I had gotten there under the power of my own two legs.

But the secret, I realized, wasn't in my legs. It wasn't in my body at all. The secret was sitting right next to me, looking up at that same perfect blue sky framed by magnificent red rock. The reality was, if I had kept this idea to myself, I probably would never have followed through. The reason I was here at all was because I had an enabler of the best kind in Heidi—someone who egged me on, refusing to let me make excuses or play it safe.

My friendship with Heidi isn't normal. Then again, most runner friendships aren't. Where most friends would say, "Poor baby," running friends say, "You're *being* a baby." Where most friends offer gentle encouragement, running friends talk smack. Running buddies celebrate the best, tolerate the worst, and pretend not to notice the embarrassing. They're a vault for the secrets that we share on the trail, when we're hungry, hot, and way too tired to be anything but 100 percent real. And when someone asks, "Would it be a horrible idea if . . . ?" the running buddy's answer is always, "Yes. What time?" A running buddy sees your limitless potential and will happily act as a mirror until you see it, too.

"Ready to go?" Heidi asked, splashing the water playfully and snapping me out of my contemplation. I wanted to stay on that shoreline forever, but it was time to climb—coming up was *mandatory* after all. We slid back into our socks and shoes, slung our bags over our shoulders, and took off for the top.

Climbing the switchbacks to get out of the canyon offered the same breathtaking views as going down but with significantly more time to appreciate them. It's slow and steep—some might even call it a slog—and yet every time we stopped to catch our breath, we couldn't help but look at each other and remark on just how damn cool it was.

As we got closer to the top, we slowly reintegrated into civilization. More and more day hikers began to appear. We passed children licking ice cream cones, and we unabashedly photobombed tourist selfies with our salt-encrusted faces. "Did you do the whole thing?" they asked, taking stock of our dust-streaked faces and sweat-soaked clothes. "Yes," we said proudly. "We absolutely did."

"What's it like down there?" they wanted to know. What's awesome is that, for the rest of our lives, Heidi and I will be in the 1 percent of people who can answer that question. To be able to wear that distinction is more satisfying than any finisher's medal.

A pickup truck arrived to shuttle us back to our campsite. We climbed in the bed of the truck and propped ourselves against the back window, feeling the deep fatigue pool into our muscles.

"We did it," I said. It still didn't seem real.

"Of course we did," Heidi replied, putting up a tired hand for a fist bump. "We're awesome."

As the truck turned off the main drag onto a dirt road, we took in the view one more time. The canyon looked different now, smaller. I turned to grin at Heidi.

"I think we should do Zion National Park next," I said. "There's a 50-mile trail there that—"

"Dammit, Susan," Heidi said with a chuckle, shaking her head in disbelief. "Can I at least take a shower before you rope me into something else?"

I laughed and put my hands up, nodding in submission. As the truck rumbled down the dirt road, we sat for awhile in silent satisfaction, taking in the enormity of what we had just done. Heidi rested her head on my shoulder and sighed.

"Zion, huh? Tell me more."

TRAINING BUDDIES MANIFESTO

Finding the perfect training partner is a challenge. It's not enough to have someone who matches your speed; you also have to find someone whose company you enjoy over lots of miles. I have plenty of friends perfect for a dinner party or a coffee chat, but if I had to share a 16-mile run through the desert with some of those same people, it's highly likely only one of us would return to the trailhead.

My training partners are some of my most cherished friends. Over our shared miles, we've celebrated, mourned, bullshitted, chastised, chased, been chased, gotten lost, and made profound discoveries. Even after all that, they *still* allow me to be seen in public with them.

There are some fundamental tenets of a relationship between running partners—rules that don't typically apply to friendships "on the outside" (read: in the nonrunning world).

So, reader, behold! I give you the manifesto of training partners everywhere.

> Anything you say to me during hard intervals or hill repeats cannot be held against you. This includes obscenities, death wishes, and insults of the "your mom" variety.

> If we are racing and I pass you, I reserve the right to smack you on the bum without warning. Don't want that to happen? You best run faster.

> From time to time, I may show up in mismatched knee socks, shirts with yellowed pit stains, or shorts with holes. Don't ask questions. Just go with it.

> If our plan is to run 6 miles together, we will run 6 miles together. Even if you're dragging ass that day. Even if I'm being a whiny brat that day.

> I will not give unsolicited training advice. You will not give unsolicited training advice. We will talk shit about those who give unsolicited training advice.

> If you believe you can do it, I believe you can do it.

> When your self-doubt creeps in, I will still believe you can do it.

> I will not speak of your accidental, yet sonorous, butt toots. You will not judge me for my thigh jiggle.

> The secrets you share on the trail are safe with me. (By the way, that thing I told you during last week's 14-miler? Thanks for not making your judgy face.)

> I will be genuinely happy for you when you have the best race of your life.

> If you have the worst race of your life, I will bring cupcakes to your pity party, validate your excuses, and stroke your ego for

48 hours. After that, I will lovingly tell you to quit your bitching and forge ahead.

> If you use Google to diagnose your running injury before your doctor's appointment (even though I very explicitly told you not to), I promise to come over and close your laptop before you become convinced amputation is imminent.

> I will never, under any circumstance, steal a bite of your post-run pancakes when you aren't looking.

> There will be days when I'd rather hit the snooze button, bail on our planned track workout in favor of happy hour, or just be lazy. And I'd know you would understand. But I won't do that; I will run with you anyway.

9

FEELS LIKE HOME

"**UM . . . UH . . . ER . . .**" The clerk at Target stuttered and stammered, looking at me with a mix of fear and confusion.

"Yes?" I smiled encouragingly.

We stared at each other in silence for a moment, and then suddenly, as if jolted by jumper cables, she yelped and skittered down the aisle: "LET ME GET MY MANAGER!" she shouted over her shoulder.

Minutes later, the clerk returned with a woman in an official-looking headset and sweater-vest. With exaggerated gestures and pronounced enunciation, the woman offered her assistance.

"I UNDERSTAND [*points to self, then forehead*] YOU ARE DEAF! [*points to ears*] HOW [*shrugs shoulders*] CAN I [*points to self*] HELP YOU [*points at me*]?"

This interaction in Target was the third of its kind that morning, each one stranger than the last. A few hours earlier, I had been interrupted midorder at Starbucks by the young cashier who, upon noticing my hearing aid, pointed and barked, "Hey! You got one of those things in your ear!" While signing up for a library card, I was asked repeatedly whether I needed a sign language interpreter, which I repeatedly declined. "Are you *sure*?" the librarian offered for the fifth time in as many minutes. "We can get one here in 15 minutes!" She was so excited about being able to offer the service, I almost felt guilty telling her I lip-read and don't actually *know* sign language.

In the Target parking lot, I wiped away frustrated tears and sent a text message to Neil: I'm pretty sure I'm the first deaf person in Utah.

Normally, I don't get discouraged by such interactions. For the most part, I've embraced being deaf and the unique opportunity I have to dispel stereotypes about the deaf and hard-of-hearing. But that day, I didn't want to dispel stereotypes. I didn't want to be unique. I didn't want to embrace a damn thing. I just wanted to have *one* human interaction that left me feeling . . . well, human.

It's always a risk when I open my mouth to talk to a stranger. I'm never quite sure how people will respond to my deaf accent.

Usually, there's a brief moment of recognition—*Hey, something's not quite right here*—followed by adjustment: *She's deaf. Okay, cool.* Even Neil admits this was the case when he met me. The way he tells the story, the first time he spotted me at a race, he made cartoony *a-OO-gah!* eyes. He wanted to know my name and if he could take me out for a cup of coffee sometime.

"Then you started talking, and I was like, *What's wrong with her?*" Neil says of that first interaction. "And then it hit me that nothing was wrong. You just had a hearing aid." Neil shrugs. "I thought, *Oh, cool. I'd still tap that.*"

It's not the "meet cute" of Hollywood rom-coms, I know. Still, it makes me swoon—not for the tapping sentiment (though that is a nice plus), but because I didn't even know this story until after we got married four years later. From my side, I only saw a good-looking guy who wasn't fazed by the deaf thing—because a lot of people are.

It was particularly hard when I moved from my safe haven in Arizona, where everyone knew me, to Utah, where I didn't know a soul. Shortly after we married, Neil accepted a four-year assignment in Utah; we sold our home in Phoenix and moved to Salt Lake City. People warned me that Utah might be a challenging place to live. After all, the majority of the population is Mormon, members of a religion that has been satirized for everything from its door-to-door evangelism to its strange rule forbidding drinks warmer than room temperature. All that sounded a little weird, but then again, I worship at the church of the long run, pray for tailwinds, and take communion with slimy foods in foil packages. I could handle weird.

Or so I thought. While settling into our new house in Salt Lake City, I tried to befriend my new neighbors the only way I knew how: asking someone on the train about the race shirt she was wearing or going out of my way at the grocery store to ask the guy in split shorts for local trail recommendations. The responses were confused looks, nervous laughter, and the slow, fearful "don't make eye contact" backward walk usually reserved for mountain lions.

At first, I let it roll off my back, thinking these responses were just flukes. But the more it happened, the more I started to isolate myself. Instead of going to the grocery store, where the clerk had once asked me how I communicated with others if I was deaf (my deadpan response: "What do you think we're doing right now?"), I ordered provisions online. Instead of checking out the cool local coffee shop that had just opened down the street, I went to Starbucks, where I could order my coffee from an app and didn't have to risk an embarrassing interaction. When we went on a dinner date, Neil ordered for the both of us—not out of chivalry, mind you, but because nothing ruins the ambiance of a quiet, romantic restaurant faster than a waitress yelling and fake-signing at a deaf customer. The only time I left my house was to go on campus to teach, where my students were obliged to stay put, despite their obvious initial shock at my accent on the first day of class.

Running became my safety raft in this ocean of weird. For a few hours each day, I could leave my house and not worry about uncomfortable interactions. A smile or a nod in passing with another runner offers little opportunity for awkwardness or confusion. But let's face it, a smile or nod is not a post-run coffee with a friend, nor is it smack talk with a training buddy. I was lonely.

Even as the roads and trails of Utah became more familiar, I found myself wondering whether Salt Lake would ever feel like home. When the feelings of isolation were especially intense, I'd run to a nearby park, popular with runners for the 1-mile dirt track that encircled the grounds, and merge into the paceline. I yearned for my running community in Phoenix, where "You're a runner? Me, too! Let's be friends!" is a perfectly acceptable opening line and where my disability went largely unnoticed, because, as my friend Dan once put it, "We're all a little bit off here, yo."

On a particularly difficult day, after a colleague made a comment about how my husband is "obviously a good man if he married a deaf woman," I was heading to the paceline in the park to burn off some steam. In the long sun of the late afternoon, I noticed a shadow that wasn't mine. The shadow persisted for a full block until a stoplight required us both to pause.

"Hey!" I heard beside me. A fellow runner, a woman about my age, took out one earbud and flashed a warm smile.

"Hey," I returned the smile.

"You heading to Liberty Park?"

"Yeah."

"Cool. Me, too."

The crosswalk signal changed and off we went.

I didn't know who the woman was. I didn't know her name, what race she was training for, or where she lived in my neighborhood. I didn't know if she noticed that I was deaf or if she even cared. All I knew was that after weeks of feeling like a mutant, that three-second connection—a variation of "You're a runner? Me, too!"—was the first time I had felt normal in Salt Lake City.

Later that week, a local magazine contacted me to ask if I was willing to pick up a freelance assignment. They wanted a story on the Salt Lake City Marathon, which had a colorful history involving a dodgy Harold Hill–style race director who skipped town just weeks before the first event. Thanks to the collective efforts of runners in Utah, the marathon was saved.

While researching the story, I discovered that the Salt Lake City Marathon finish line was just a block from my house, on a familiar stretch of road between Library Square and City Hall. Shortly after filing the article with my editor, I opened the registration website and secured a spot in the race. It was so convenient—I could literally stumble across the street after finishing. No weird interactions with anyone, no awkward attempts to order food on the drive home—it was perfect.

I hadn't expected those 26.2 miles to be anything special. After all, I ran segments of the course just about every day: up

Capitol Hill, through Memory Grove Park, past the Mormon temple, around the campus where I taught. But I had forgotten about the alchemy of race day, where ordinary roads become something special. For me, on that day, those everyday routes morphed into a side of Salt Lake City I hadn't seen before. From the moment I boarded the shuttle to the start line until the moment I crossed the finish, I was, for the first time, part of the community. Runners offered encouragement and high fives. Volunteers handed me cups of water and seemed genuinely excited for my progress. Spectators cheered for me by name, and even though they only knew it because **SUSAN** was emblazoned on my bib in bold letters, my heart swelled every time someone said it out loud. *Yes! That's right! I have a name! And it's not "the deaf one"!*

On race day, no one knew I was different. For the first time since moving to Salt Lake City, I felt like I was one of them. They had no idea how much I needed that moment of recognition. Until that race, neither did I.

Since then, I've signed up every year for one of the races at the Salt Lake City Marathon. And so, even though I had sworn I wouldn't do any traditional or familiar races during my year of running outside my comfort zone, I made this one exception to join the masses moving through my 'hood. Though I always retreat back to my isolated ways the next day, somehow that race gives me a booster shot that makes the rest of the year more tolerable. On days when I need a little more, I run to Liberty Park and hop in the paceline.

Before my first Salt Lake City Marathon, I don't think I had fully grasped how much power each of us wields. With a smile, a wave, or even just a nod, we can change the course of another person's day. Every path we cross, however briefly, is an opportunity to choose kindness. We may not know if the other person needs it, but then again, do we really have to know? We can choose kindness anyway.

My time in Salt Lake is coming to an end soon. After Neil completes his assignment, he and I will return to Arizona, where his company's US headquarters is located. After four years, Utah still doesn't feel like home, and I don't think it ever will. But that's okay, because I've learned how to find community in pacelines and small kindnesses.

When I pack my boxes and return to Arizona, I probably won't need my safety raft anymore. If anyone else needs it, you're welcome to hop on.

I promise, there's plenty of room.

26.2 LIFE LESSONS FROM THE MARATHON

Every time I run a marathon, two things crisscross my mind throughout the race: One, marathons are stupid. Why do I keep doing this to myself? Two, marathons are amazing. Why don't I do this more often?

I alternate between those sentiments over the course of 26.2 miles, and one or the other usually wins out by the finish line. Most of the time, I rejoice with my hands up in the air, wanting to do it all over again. Sometimes, though, it's the "marathons are stupid" voice that takes precedence, and I swear to *never, ever, ever* run 26.2 consecutive miles again.

So why, if marathons are so stupid, do I keep doing this to myself? Hell if I know. Madam Marathon has her claws in me, and try as I may to shake her off, I can't.

And I'm okay with that. For as stupid as marathons are, they've actually made me smarter. Training for and racing a marathon is a transformative experience—mind, body, and spirit—and I find that when I move, my self-awareness needle moves. When I move a lot, as is required for 26.2 miles, my self-awareness needle moves a lot.

As a result, the lessons from Madam Marathon make me a better person in all aspects of my life. Maybe that's why I keep doing this to myself—because I'm not done learning yet. Or maybe I'm just an idiot who doesn't know when to say no. But I'm an idiot in progress— that's got to count for something, right?

At any rate, I'm learning, I'm growing, and by golly, I'm still running. What I've learned along the way:

1   **The first step is often the hardest.** It's one thing to say, "I want to run a marathon." It's an entirely different thing to follow through and sign up.

2   **If you want to do it, you have to do it.** People can bullshit their way through a lot of things in life. The marathon is not one of those things.

3   **Fear takes you places.** And I'm not just talking about the finish line.

4   **Your body is damn impressive.** It's hard to bemoan your jiggly thighs when they just carried you 26.2 miles.

5   **You know less than you know.** Just when you think you've gotten this running thing nailed, something comes along and makes you feel like a moron. Who knew there were life lessons in skinned knees and low glycogen?

6   **Nobody really knows anything, anyway.** It's not just you. We're all just trying to figure it out.

7   **Failure is a success.** You screwed up? Good for you! That means you tried, you learned, and you grew.

8 **Bad weather is no excuse.** Neither is a poor night's sleep, a dead iPod battery, a long day at work, or a Disney movie marathon.

9 **Running will not solve all your problems.** It's really just one kind of pain to distract you from another kind of pain. But it is a much better kind of pain.

10 **If your paleo / gluten-free / vegan diet or your minimalist / maximalist / bubble wrap shoes have rocked your world, awesome!** Talk about it! Just don't get too preachy. People tend to tune that out.

11 **Your strength may be your weakness, so beware.** You can climb any hill, power through any speed session, and suffer like a champ. You're also too strong for rest days and too stubborn to admit when you're injured.

12 **Joy is a rocket.** Little boosts of speed come from the corners of your smile. So thank the volunteers, high-five that excited toddler, and laugh heartily at spectator signs.

13 **Someone always has it worse than you.** Every time you think you're suffering more than anyone in the history of suffering has ever suffered, the Endurance Gods will place someone in your path who's been through more and is overcoming it.

14 **You can be a badass and a dumbass simultaneously.** Case in point: At mile 22, you said, "You go, girl!" to encourage a fellow runner. He had a mustache.

15 **Look at the path, not the obstacles.** It's all about perspective.

16 **Appearances can be deceiving.** The person you least expect to see in a marathon is often the most inspiring.

17 **You do you.** Don't look to other people as a gauge for your success. The comparison trap is a nasty one.

18 **It's good to disconnect.** In a hyper-plugged-in society, enjoy the pleasure of telling someone, "You called? Sorry, I was running."

19 **Ask for help.** You don't have to go it alone.

20 **Be open.** Running will transform you. But the transformation you want isn't always the transformation you need.

21 **26.2 miles is a long way.** For real.

22   **Just say it.** At some point in every marathon, surrender to the fact that yes, 26.2 miles is a long way; yes, this is uncomfortable; yes, this kind of sucks. It's okay—even healthy—to admit that.

23   **"I can't go on" is a lie.** You totally can go on, you sissy.

24   **Simplify.** This ain't rocket science. Fancy gizmos can complicate something that doesn't require complication.

25   **Look up.** While you are lamenting your tired feet or cursing your GPS watch, you might miss a most spectacular view.

26   **Don't wait until the finish line to celebrate.** Embrace the little victories along the way. Sometimes they mean more than the finisher's medal.

26.2   **But damn, that finisher's medal is pretty cool, too.**

10

ONE MILE AT A TIME

I'D ALWAYS THOUGHT OF THE ROAD MILE as the redheaded stepchild of racing. Unlike track and field, which gets all the TV coverage during the Olympic games, and the marathon, which is seen as the ultimate bucket-list challenge to aspire to, the mile always just seemed kind of . . . there. People minimize the race all the time—it's "just" a mile, after all. What could possibly be so hard about it? Just about anyone can run a mile if they really want to, including your Uncle Ed after saying, "Here, hold my beer."

Besides, the mile sucks. Ask anyone who has taken a phys ed class, and they'll likely recall some sort of early traumatic experience with the mile race. For me, it was the President's Challenge, a middle school rite of passage that was part NFL Scouting Combine, part child abuse. Every year, our gym teacher, Mrs. Morey, pulled us out of our regularly scheduled programming of kickball and square dance lessons, announcing it was time to test our fitness as Americans. And every year, said prepubescent Americans would groan and wonder if they could sneak out to get a doctor's note.

But, no! There would be no skipping out on the President's Challenge! Mrs. Morey made that clear: "The President's Challenge is what separates the eagles from the turkeys! Only turkeys get doctor's notes! Now, everybody go stand in line and wait your turn to dangle from the pull-up bar!"

I could never do a pull-up, by the way. My sit-ups weren't all that impressive, either. I did nail that sit-and-reach, though. If there were two things I was good at, it was sitting and reaching.

The pinnacle of the President's Challenge was the 1-mile run. This was also Mrs. Morey's favorite. Not because she was a runner, mind you—her sport of choice was bowling—but because it was the one day of the year when she could stand with her megaphone on the hill behind the school and blare, "YAY, EAGLES! BOOOOOOOO, TURKEYS!" She couldn't do that in the gym, which was within earshot of the principal's office. Principals tend to frown upon that kind of thing.

In case it isn't already obvious from my salty recollections, I was very much a turkey. Despite its intent of inspiring kids to strive for better fitness and faster times, the President's Challenge was, for me, an awful, demeaning experience that only served to push me further away from exercise. After graduation, I avoided running because of it, and even when I did give running another try in adulthood, there was *no freaking* way I was going to do the mile.

At first, this avoidance was purely due to my President's Challenge PTSD. However, the more I got into running, the more I understood that racing a mile was really, really far out of my comfort zone.

The marathon is like a fine cognac; it's not something you imbibe every day. On those special occasions when you do open the bottle, you savor every moment. You swish the amber liquid around in your glass, smell its robust aroma, and relish the complexity of each sip.

Racing the mile, on the other hand, is basically a shaken bottle of pink champagne: wild, effervescent, and bound to explode all over your good shoes. It goes down fast, leaving you feeling tipsy and giggly. And sometimes, it makes you puke in the neighbor's bushes.

When it comes to running, I'm decidedly a cognac gal. I'd rather savor my time on the trails. Nothing makes me happier than taking in the sights, sounds, and smells of my surroundings during a long run. Even my work as a running journalist has always focused on the endurance side of the sport, with a distinct preference for covering marathons and long-course triathlons. I understand those kinds of races and the people who do them. The mile? That's for crazy people.

So, of course, I found myself on an assignment in Iowa, covering the USA Track and Field 1 Mile Road Championships. And, of course, I found myself entering its amateur counterpart, the Grand Blue Mile.

The Grand Blue Mile is part of the Drake Relays, one of the most prestigious track-and-field events in the United States. Every April, the running world descends upon Drake University in Des Moines, Iowa, for a celebration of all things running. Amateur, collegiate, and professional runners alike head to the iconic "Blue Oval" to test their mettle in classic track-and-field events. The 40,000 spectators also have plenty of other competitions to watch, including an indoor pole-vaulting competition and a bulldog beauty pageant to select the perfect smushy face to serve as the event's mascot. (I can verify that the 2018 winner, a two-year-old English bulldog named Bow-Z, who gamely let me bombard him with kisses and schmoompy-woompy talk, is indeed a very good boy.)

The kickoff to all these shenanigans is the Grand Blue Mile. Unlike the headlining four-lap event, which takes place on the Drake University track later in the week (purists note that it is 1,600 meters and not a "real" American mile, which is about 9.3 meters longer), the road mile event is a frenetic dash through the streets of downtown Des Moines. Instead of track's protocol of heats and designated lanes, a road mile is a one-shot, every-runner-for-herself throwdown.

I wasn't sure what to expect when I landed in Des Moines. A tiny part of me feared that Mrs. Morey and her bullhorn would greet me in the airport terminal. After all, there was a lot of turkey potential in this trip. In addition to racing the road mile for the first time, I was also covering a track event for the first time. I barely recognized a handful of names on the professional roster, and I certainly wasn't able to match any of those names to a face. All I could do was make notes on a printout of the start list and hope I didn't screw up in cross-referencing bib numbers.

Because of a wonky Wi-Fi connection in my hotel, I decided to tuck into a coffee shop for a few hours to prepare for that evening's coverage. While I was scrolling through information on the Drake Relays on my laptop, someone tapped her fingers on the empty chair across from me.

"Is this seat taken?" the woman asked.

"No," I replied. "Go ahead."

"Thanks," she said, placing her coffee cup on the table and sinking into the overstuffed chair. "It's crazy in here."

As she sipped her latte and scrolled through her phone, I noted all the signs of an elite runner—lithe body, new shoes, jacket emblazoned with sponsor logos.

"Are you racing at Drake this week?" I asked.

"Just tonight. The mile."

"Me, too!" I exclaimed.

She cocked her head, clearly a little confused.

"Oh, I mean the amateur event, not the championship race," I clarified. Explaining that I was in town to write about the professional race, I shared with her that I was also spending a year doing races outside my comfort zone. As someone who preferred endurance events, I definitely included the mile in that category.

"Thank you for saying that!" she exulted, raising her arms in gleeful victory. "Everyone thinks the mile is easy."

"I've heard that sentiment, yes."

"It's not!"

"I agree."

"But between you and me," she leaned in closer, lowering her voice to a stage whisper, "I'll take a mile over a marathon any day. Anything over a 5K is insane."

I laughed as she downed the last of her coffee and stood up. "Nice meeting you," she said, smiling. "Good luck tonight."

"You, too."

As I watched her walk away, I processed what had just taken place. Two runners with vastly different perspectives—one who was scared of running a singular mile and one who thought it ridiculous to run 26.2 of them. Which is a scarier race? Which one hurts more? Which one is more impressive? It comes down to perspective, that seemed clear. But somehow, knowing that I routinely did something a badass professional runner thought was hard gave me a major confidence boost. I packed up my laptop, went back to my hotel to change, and headed out to give it my all at the Grand Blue Mile.

I had assumed that people would consider a mile race as boring as I had back in gym class. That assumption went double for a mile race in Des Moines, Iowa, a town that, while charming in its own way, doesn't have the most exciting reputation. So I was all the more dumbfounded to arrive at the event and discover a massive crowd. Who were all these people? Nearly 3,000 people had signed up to race the mile that evening, and even more had come out to watch. There were bright lights, loud cheers, and a course that cut through tall buildings and under pedestrian bridges. It was fresh. It was sexy. It was thrilling. It was absolutely the opposite of what I had expected from a mile race in downtown Des Moines.

It was also really, really hard. As with any running race, the biggest challenge of the mile is pacing. But this was no ordinary race for me. I was comfortable with the slow, familiar trickle of a marathon, dealing with pain in measured doses. In the mile, a starting gun fires, and the whole field springs forward as if it had been launched from the pistol itself. The crowd blurs. The mouth dries. The legs burn. You start out thinking, *It's just a mile.* But believe this, reader, you will never utter that phrase again. The mile is fucking painful. It was the longest short race I'd ever done; seconds felt like minutes, and minutes felt like hours because *Holy hell, I can't hold on any longer.*

As far as finish times go, mine was solidly in turkey territory. I sprint like an endurance athlete, which is to say, I don't really sprint. My all-out mile, as it turns out, is the same as the pace my husband averages for a marathon. Still, I didn't feel like a turkey. Pushing my body to the limit like that made me feel like a goddamned eagle. And as I crossed that finish line, gassed and shell-shocked, my very first thought was *If only Mrs. Morey could see me now.*

Sometimes, it's good to put down that familiar snifter of cognac, run in a champagne race, and let it explode all over your good shoes. I did, indeed, find myself tipsy and giggly at the end of the Grand Blue Mile. I also felt like puking in the neighbor's bushes. But I also got to experience running in a new way, one that was painful and uncomfortable in its own way but also incredibly cool. And while I'm not going to be throwing down at track meets anytime soon, I have been complaining a little less during interval workouts. "It's just a mile" has become "It's not as hard as *the* mile."

I wish I had gotten the name of the runner I met in the coffee shop that day. Though I caught a glimpse of her in the professional race, which took place after the amateur heats, she disappeared while I was interviewing the winner for a story. It's too bad—I'd love to invite her to do a marathon someday.

After all, a little perspective can go a long, long way.

LAY IT ALL BARE

THE CALIENTE SUBDIVISION in Land O' Lakes, Florida, is like any other neighborhood in the Sunshine State. Take a right past the entry gate, and there's a row of pastel-painted stucco homes, where smiling residents sit on their lanais, drinking coffee. Continue on down the road, and you'll come upon a man-made lake with a middle-aged couple power walking along its shores. When you pass by a block of townhouses, an elderly Japanese man waves to you as he waters his potted plants with a garden hose.

It's a lovely setting, which makes it all the more jarring when you notice that one of the coffee-drinking neighbors has nipples the size of saucers and that the power-walking couple have matching compass tattoos on their upper left thighs. Also, that plant-watering neighbor is wielding more than one garden hose, if you catch my drift.

They say you're not supposed to stare at people in a nudist community. I'm not sure how that's possible, because everywhere you turn, there's another dick, schlong, twink, or tally-whacker, and . . . *how do you not look?* It's impossible.

"It's just the human body; it's just the human body," I repeated to myself as I pulled into a parking spot outside the main building. "Totally natural."

A short, redheaded man crossed the road in front of my car, wearing a black, sleeveless T-shirt with white block letters blaring ROCK OUT WITH YOUR COCK OUT. With no pants on, he was doing just that.

"Hello!" he called, with a friendly wave. I smiled with the awkward, clenched-jaw smile that comes when you don't know who someone is, but you do know his metaphorical carpet matches the drapes.

"Who am I kidding?" I muttered as I returned his wave. "There is nothing natural about this day."

I had so many questions about racing in the Caliente Bare Dare 5K: Did I have to go completely nude? How was I supposed to keep my knockers from knocking? Where did my race number go? Should I have scheduled a bikini wax?

And the biggest question of all: Was this going to be some kind of sordid, creepy peep show? In my head, the people who did naked runs were either perverts who still lived in their mom's basement or the porn stars who starred in the videos downloaded by said basement-dwelling perverts.

"I hear that a lot," Pete Williams laughed when I contacted him about the race ahead of my arrival in Florida. "I promise, it's not what you think."

Pete is the race director of the Caliente Bare Dare 5K, which also bills itself as the National Championship of Nude Running. Admittedly, it doesn't have the same elite status as other championship events—no qualifying races are needed to toe the line in Caliente. The only prerequisite is a willingness to show up and strip down. But as far as naked 5Ks go (surprisingly, there are several opportunities around the United States to sprint in the buff), Caliente's is the largest and most renowned, with an average of 350 runners representing 25 states each year.

Unlike traditional road races, where the finish line is the focus, naked running is more about the "nakation," or experiencing the freedom of a nudist lifestyle, said Pete. People arrive with the expectation that they'll run the race and, afterward, quickly put their clothes back on and go home. But many end up staying once they realize that clothing-optional resorts have really nice people and really fun activities. Naturists, or social nudists, tend to be pretty chill, he said.

The culture prides itself on being positive, authentic, and openhearted—or, as one Caliente resident described it, "We're free-range humans." The nudist resort, I would come to learn, is more hippie commune than cheesy porn film. For nudists, shedding clothes is a way of removing the pretensions of society, accepting people for who they are, and being more present in the world.

"In other races, people leave not long after crossing the finish line. Here, people stay all day or even all week," Pete said, explaining that most naked 5Ks are part of bigger, open-house-style events, with camping, music, and sporting events held at resorts that are typically restricted to members only. The finish-line pool party at the Caliente Bare Dare is particularly notorious in the naturist world, Pete pointed out, with music, dancing, and the opportunity for visiting runners and triathletes to even out their awkward tan lines.

"Wait," I said, surprised by this revelation. "Visiting runners and triathletes?"

"We get a lot of them," Pete nodded. Though the majority of residents at Caliente are active individuals, there aren't too many naked runners living in the subdivision. Most of the competitors at the Bare Dare are outsiders who arrive for the bucket-list experience of freeballing in a 5K. Perhaps not surprisingly, the race typically sees a 65 to 35 percent split between genders, which is in line with the naturist community at large. In general, men tend to outnumber women at naturist events and clubs, as they're simply more likely to feel free when au naturel. Unlike women, who tend to scrutinize everything that's wrong with their bodies, men are more likely to look in a mirror with a wink and an air-gun: "Looking good, stud."

This gender split is what I noticed most as I sat in my parked car, watching athletes make their way from their vehicles to race registration—the Caliente Bare Dare was a real sausage fest. Although women were participating in the race, there were a lot more men, their wieners wagging to and fro as they did warm-up jogs in the parking lot.

Before arriving, I had been nervous about the carnal con-notation of a nudist resort. With all the naked people running around, wouldn't it be a sexually charged environment? Was it inappropriate for me to attend the race without my husband, who is technically the only person allowed to see me naked? I had asked him not to come with me that weekend. It was bad enough my tits would be flapping in the wind; I didn't want any-one I knew to witness it.

But observing the typical pre-race rituals in the parking lot of a nudist resort made me realize there was nothing arousing about seeing runners do hamstring stretches and toe touches naked. It was far from sexy; if anything, it was a little silly, and I found myself giggling. Just then, a pack of nude runners walked past my car on their way to race registration, and my giggling stopped. As the only person in the parking lot wearing clothes, I was actually the silly one.

Though it's not required to disrobe completely, more than 90 percent of the runners at the Caliente Bare Dare do. The remaining 10 percent wear very little—a sports bra or a jock-strap, perhaps, or a pair of thong underwear. A few women wore tasseled pasties for festive flair. All runners wore shoes; though clothing is optional at the Caliente Bare Dare, footwear is not.

I cursed silently, looking down at the shorts and tank top I had arrived in. Feeling suddenly massively overdressed, I took a deep breath, slouched down low in my seat, and wriggled out of my clothing. Even though everything about a naked run was silly, it was also intimidating. This wasn't watching TV in my under-wear at home with the shades drawn; this was going out for the world to see everything about me. *Everything.* The cellulite on my ass, scars I had collected over the years, curves and lumps and bumps I had gotten adept at concealing with clothing—it was all going to be out there in the open.

It was a full five minutes before I finally opened the door to my car, and another minute before I got the nerve to stand up. My legs shook as I walked away from the protection of my car, with nothing to hide behind but a pair of sunglasses.

"Heading to the start?" A sturdy, muscular man fell into step alongside me.

I nodded, trying to avoid a glimpse of his trouser snake.

He extended his arm for a handshake. "My name's Rob. What's yours?"

"Susan."

"Hey!" Rob exclaimed. "My mom's name is Susan!" He continued to tell me about his mom. I think he said she lives in Louisiana, but I was having a hard time paying attention, because I was too busy adjusting to the parallel universe in which it's completely normal to strike up a conversation with someone who is not wearing any clothes.

It rapidly became clear to me that jovial chats were standard at a naked run. In fact, the more people I encountered, the more I realized that nudists were *really* good conversationalists. Never had I been in a situation where people so aggressively tried to maintain eye contact and ask follow-up questions to keep the dialogue going. Was it an intentional move (*don't-look-at-her-tits-don't-look-at-her-tits*)? Were we trying to avoid awkward silences, which would require us to look around at the sea of schlongs? Had clothes been distracting us from human connection all along? Was it just a collective effort to put each other at ease in our bizarre new, pants-free world? I wasn't sure, but weirdly, I kind of liked it.

Other surreal normalcies of my new parallel universe:

> Racing without a bib number: "Where would you pin them?" Pete asked.

> A wall of snow-white butt cheeks as 350 runners turned to salute the flag for the "Star-Spangled Banner"

> Extreme courtesy after the starting gun: No one throws elbows to jockey for position at a naked race, because who knows where said elbow will land.

> The observation that fake boobs don't bounce
> The (painful) confirmation that I definitely do not have fake boobs
> A tattoo of an X with "Your lips here" on a racer's right butt cheek: I liked him immediately.
> A diverse display of hirsutism
> Vajazzling—so much vajazzling

What was most surprising, though, was how much a naked 5K was really like any other 5K. There were (naked) volunteers handing out cups of water, (naked) course marshals directing traffic, and (naked) spectators along the race with signs like **GRIN AND BARE IT** and **GO NUDIES!** There were even (naked) residents honking the horns of their golf carts, because they were a little peeved that our race was holding up traffic on their way to (naked) yoga class at the Caliente Fitness Center.

Once I got used to the elasticity of my own body (and promised to never take a sports bra for granted again), I settled into a rhythm, racing in the same way I would any other 5K. Only this time, instead of trying to pick off the woman in the red shirt ahead of me, I set my sights on the lady with a lower-back tattoo of an atom. When I passed her, I chased down the guy with the wonky birthmark on his right shoulder. Naked racing is just racing, with 75 percent more bouncy parts.

In a day of surprises, what was most surprising of all? I set a 5K PR. We could credit it to my increased training that year or perhaps the aerodynamic advantage of running in the nude, but the truth is that I really, really wanted to beat the girl with the fake knockers. I'm sure she's a lovely person, but it made me irrationally irritated that her boobs stayed high and firm, while mine flopped all over the place like a pair of inflatable wahoos outside of a car dealership. Don't judge me—the inspiration to dig deep sometimes comes from strange places, okay?

For the record, I didn't beat her. But I still won, in my own way. When I crossed the finish line in PR time, a (naked) volunteer handed me a card with the number 10 on it.

"Congratulations!" she cheered. "You can pick up your prize at the awards table!"

"I'm sorry, what?" I squinted at the card.

"Your prize!" She pointed at the number 10. "Take it over there and tell them you got 10th place!"

Reader, my joyful victory salute, arms pumping as I reached high into the heavens, was so vigorous, I actually pulled my pectoral muscle. The fun of explaining this to my Utah-conservative Mormon doctor was worth every penny of my insurance co-pay. Even now, a year later, my left boob aches a little after long runs.

But it's fine, because if you visit my household these days, you'll see my first-ever race trophy on the mantel, which I earned for my 10th place finish in the 2018 National Championship of Nude Running. Like the Caliente community, the trophy appears perfectly normal at first glance—an unopened bottle of red wine with a bright, colorful label. Then you get a little closer, and you see a cheeky photo of a nude lady in the pool at Caliente, a pair of running shoes slung over her shoulder. It's the perfect souvenir from my "nakation."

The only thing that would make it better is a garden hose or two.

12

BACK STORY

MY YEAR OF RUNNING OUTSIDE THE COMFORT ZONE was supposed to take me to new places and new experiences. It wasn't supposed to take me back to Phoenix—and certainly not to a mountain that I had avoided so well for so long.

I was in town for a show with the USA Today Network's Storytellers Project. They were putting together a compendium of stories centered around the theme "Growing Up" and had invited me to tell a story from my first book, *Life's Too Short to Go So F*cking Slow.* It was an opportunity I couldn't refuse—Phoenix is the setting for that book, which chronicles my unlikely friendship with my boss-turned-mentor, Carlos Nunez. Phoenix is where Carlos, a 13-time Ironman competitor, interrupted my smoke break at work one day and suggested I start swimming with him instead of sucking on a cigarette. It's where he convinced me to add running to my repertoire and where he taught me how to ride a bike. It's where I got the insane idea that I could do a long-course triathlon myself, despite never having done any kind of endurance event. It's where sport became a vehicle for getting my life together. And it's where, over the course of many years and miles together, my boss became my best friend.

Phoenix is also where Carlos was diagnosed with cancer at the age of 46, where he received the treatments that made him writhe in pain, and where he inspired so many with his grace and strength in the face of a disease that aims to weaken and embitter. Phoenix is where the doctors exhausted all their options. And Phoenix is where I said goodbye to my best friend.

Moving to Salt Lake City at the time of Carlos's death provided me with a hard reset on life—a chance to adjust to the new normal without constant reminders of the way things used to be. I was sad to leave the city I loved but also relieved that I didn't have to live in the shadow of South Mountain, where my friendship with Carlos was cemented in heart-to-heart conversations during 100-degree trail runs and over smack talk on Sunday morning bike rides.

Whenever I returned to the desert to visit friends and family, I'd pack my schedule with all my favorite people and places—

enchiladas at my favorite hole-in-the-wall, long conversations over coffee, a workout with my favorite Masters swim group. But if anyone suggested, "Hey, how about a trail run at South Mountain?" I'd recoil. I just couldn't do it. There was too much history there.

Most of my visits to Phoenix lasted only a day or two, just enough time to get my fix and get out before I could be hit with a wave of sentimentality. For the Storytellers show, however, I was back for a week. In between rehearsals, I hit up all my favorite spots with all my favorite people. This trip offered a particularly special reunion, as Carlos's daughters, Claudia and Emily, were graduating from college that same weekend. I was thrilled to be there to celebrate an accomplishment their father had talked about for so long. At their graduation party, I told the girls the story of how one day, during a trail run on South Mountain, Carlos confessed that he was nervous about his kids going to college.

"Why?" I asked him. "They're intelligent kids. They're going to do great."

"Exactly! They already *think* they're smarter than me," said Carlos, who held a doctorate in engineering. "But now they're going to *know* they are."

The kids loved hearing a story about their dad they hadn't heard before. "I wish he were here," Emily said. "I miss him." Claudia wrapped an arm around Emily and their teenage brother, Andrew. They had shown such grace and maturity, even through such a devastating loss. Carlos would have been so proud.

I smiled sadly. "Me, too."

My bittersweet week continued in rehearsals for the Storytellers Project, where I worked and reworked the combination of words in hopes of finding the right ones. It felt impossible. How do you condense a decade of profound, life-changing friendship into only 10 minutes? I regretted signing up for the show. Everything I said felt clumsy and trite.

I had spent the past three years in Salt Lake City adjusting to my new normal, and just one week in Phoenix had taken me right back to the day Carlos died. I needed to clear my head—and fast. I changed into my running clothes, turned the key in the ignition of my rental car, and set out for Tempe Town Lake.

I drove through the streets of my old stomping grounds, past my favorite breakfast spot, and through the campus where I used to teach. I passed the first house I shared with Neil and the parking lot where I used to meet Carlos for Sunday morning bike rides. I stopped at a red light in front of Starbucks, where Carlos revealed he had stage IV cancer and only six months to live. It was the same place where we toasted to his birthday three years later, clinking together our mochas.

I was supposed to turn right at that intersection to get to the lake. Instead, I looked over my shoulder and gunned the rental car across three lanes of traffic to turn left; 20 minutes later,

I was standing in the shadow of South Mountain, trying to decide which trail I would take.

Carlos would have chosen the hardest route—he always did. But Carlos wasn't here. I looked up at the sky in defiance. "If you're going to be an asshole and make me run by myself," I snarked, "then we're taking the easy way."

I don't know if Carlos heard me. There have been times since his death when I do wonder if maybe he can. The first time was the day after he died. His wife, Diane, texted me a picture of a rainbow—at first, I thought it was just a nice picture, but then I looked closer: The rainbow was aligned perfectly with their home, as if it were pouring light and love into the family.

"I think it's him," Diane said. "I really do." She reminded me of the time Carlos said that even when he died, he wouldn't actually be gone—that, as the first law of thermodynamics states, matter can't be destroyed, only transformed. "He's still here with all of us," she smiled. "He's always going to be."

I've encountered Carlos in various forms since he died—not in ghosts or voices, but in tiny coincidences that I feel sure can only be explained by his presence. Sometimes, it's just a feeling of déjà vu. Other times, it's a more pronounced experience, like when I learned that the release date for *Life's Too Short* also happened to be the anniversary of Carlos's death. My publisher was baffled when I asked if it was an intentional choice, but she had no idea of the significance of the date. After she left the room, I looked up—just in case—and whispered, "Hello?"

So—just in case—I did it again. As I rounded the first familiar switchback of the South Mountain trail, I said hello. I also said that I was sorry it had been so long since I had met him here, but I had been so scared to come back to this place. I told him that the week had been an emotional one, and that I wished he had been there to see it all. I told him I really needed a friend.

I told him about Diane and the kids—that Claudia was starting a new job in Washington, D.C.; Emily was going to graduate school; and Andrew was talking about following in his father's footsteps by majoring in engineering when he started college next fall. "Those kids are going to change the world, you know," I said, before catching myself. Of course he knew.

I told him about the book and how the response had been so beautiful. "Everyone says they wish they had known you," I laughed. "Isn't that funny?" Carlos was the kind of guy who would have called them all dumbasses for thinking he was an inspiration. But secretly? I know he also would have loved it.

I told him about my year of misadventures, about running 50 miles in a dust storm and doing a naked 5K. I told him it was all his fault—if it weren't for him, I would never have become a runner in the first place.

I updated him on what our friends in Phoenix were up to and told him about what it was like to live in Salt Lake City. I told him I was lonely there.

The trail rounded one final corner, giving way to an overlook with views of downtown Phoenix. I sat on a rock, looking at the place that was both so familiar and so different. In the years after Carlos died, I had avoided South Mountain because I thought it would make me feel worse. When I finally came back to it, it was because I thought it would make me feel better. As it turned out, neither was the case. It was neither traumatic nor cathartic—it was just *different*.

As I reflected on the events of the past week, I kept coming back to thermodynamics: Matter isn't destroyed, only transformed. Every time I looked at Carlos's children, I saw the best parts of him. Claudia possesses his sharp intellect, Emily inherited his deep compassion, and Andrew is just as mischievous and charming as his dad. When I had met friends for a run earlier that week, some of them had brought along fresh faces—they were mentoring new runners and triathletes, just as Carlos had done with me. And every now and then, a reader lets me know that a Carlos quote from the book had gotten them through a tough race or life experience. Carlos lives on in so many ways.

"We're okay," I sniffed, wiping away a tear. "We miss you a lot, but we're doing okay."

I knew the real reason I had avoided South Mountain. It had nothing to do with the history sprinkled on the trails. It was because I knew that when I came, I'd have to acknowledge the present. Things were different now. But it was going to be okay. *We* were going to be okay.

Before I got up to head back to the trailhead, I looked up at the sky and smiled. "Thanks, sir."

That night, when I stepped into the bright lights on the stage at the Storytellers Project, I took a deep breath and looked out into the audience. Diane and the kids were there, beaming. So were some members of our running and triathlon community. And somehow, I knew, without a doubt in my mind, Carlos was there, too. I grinned and began to tell my 10-minute tale of profound, life-changing friendship.

I was smoking outside my office one day, when my boss sat down next to me . . .

SIX-WORD RUNNING STORIES

"For sale: baby shoes, never worn."

ERNEST HEMINGWAY

According to legend, Ernest Hemingway's colleagues once bet he couldn't write a complete story in only six words. He was up to the challenge, and in addition to collecting beer money for his efforts, he wrote what he considered to be "his best work ever."

I consider the USA Today Network's Storytellers Project to be my "best work ever." I've written lots of things over the years, but usually I have a lot of leeway as to what I say and how I say it. But for the show in Phoenix, I had strict rules to follow. The most important one was a 10-minute time limit.

Most of us struggle with the idea of being complete yet concise. Read any blogger's race recap, and you'll see what I mean. When someone asks, "Hey, how'd your long run go last weekend?" you'll rarely hear a runner say, "Oh, great!" No, that would be far too simple. Instead, we unleash a tale of nutrition, hydration, cramping, chafing, porta-potties, and total mileage, right down to the centimeter.

But all that is usually not necessary. The experiences and stories that come with running are universal. Some things can be conveyed with just a glance, while other things, like the runner's high, simply cannot be described with words. Our pal Ernie was right about one thing though: You can say a lot with just six words.

Marathon PR! In related news: Ow.

My running shoes are my therapists.

Runner's dilemma: to wave or not?

Night of fun; run of regret.

Post-run shower. Chafing revealed. Yikes.

Long run. Low fuel. Long walk.

Morning run. Two poops. One dog's.

Rest days are for sleeping in.

Life's meaning revealed at mile 21.

IT band massage. Pleasure and pain.

Dog thinks I'm a salt lick.

Sunday morning run and pancakes. Bliss.

I run because I can. You?

/3

STAY WEIRD,
SAN FRANCISCO

OVER THE YEARS, I'VE SEEN my fair share of interesting pre-race rituals: runners who insist on putting their right shoe on before the left, those who make the sign of the cross seconds before the gun goes off, and those who insist on wearing the same outfit for every race, right down to the socks. One friend grows a beard with every race, refusing to shave from the time he starts his training block until after he collects his finisher medal. Another follows a precise warm-up routine of exercises and stretches; if she forgets one or begins a stretch out of order, she curses loudly and starts from the beginning.

But tortilla throwing? Now that was a new one.

"YO!" shouted Dan, waving a tortilla at the crowd of runners in our midst. "Anyone got a Sharpie? I want to write my phone number on here for the ladies." Clutching the tortilla in one hand, he unzipped his fanny pack with the other, rummaging through the contents and pulling out keys, a cell phone, and a small tube of Vaseline.

"What the hell, D?" I laughed, pointing at the lotion.

"C'mon, Lacke," Dan hollered. "My junk chafes in short-shorts!" In addition to the fanny pack, Dan was sporting a barely there pair of bottoms, along with tube socks and a terry-cloth headband. "Besides," he added with a wink, "I might need it if a hot chick responds to my tortilla Tinder."

Dan flicked the tortilla into the air like a Frisbee, only to see it drop 5 feet away.

"Should've gotten corn," he said, shaking his head. "Flour doesn't fly as well."

In any other race, Dan would have been the odd man out. But at Bay to Breakers, he was just one of 40,000 wacky runners participating in the ceremonial Flinging of the Tortillas.

"What's the point of the tortillas, anyway?" I asked, ducking to avoid a flying disc.

"Who knows?" Dan laughed, picking up tortillas off the ground for another slinging. "Does it really matter?"

"Hey, Dan," Neil interjected. "Pass me the lube. My jorts are giving me chub rub." I looked over at my husband, who was tucking an old-school ringer T-shirt into his tight and tiny cutoff jean shorts. On his head, completing the retro runner ensemble, was a gloriously curly orange wig. This morning was getting stranger by the minute.

I first met Dan when we both lived in Phoenix. I heard him before I saw him, an impressive feat given that I don't hear very well. But that's the perfect introduction to Dan—no matter what the situation, his loud and larger-than-life personality enters the room before the rest of him does.

"HEY, YO!" he bellowed the first time I entered the triathlon shop where he was working. "WE GOT A NEW CUSTOMER! Welcome! What's your name? What can I do for ya? I'm Dan, and I am STOKED to meet you." I soon came to learn that if "stoke" could take a human form, it would unquestionably look like Dan.

We became fast friends, bonding over a shared love of bawdy jokes, over-the-top stories, and buttery baked goods. He was the first friend I introduced to my then-boyfriend Neil, and the two quickly developed a bromance built on long bike rides and uproarious smack talk.

Like many of our friends, Dan was a runner and triathlete who did everything from 5Ks to the major triathlons. But where he really shined was at costume runs. Whether it was donning a fat suit for a Santa Claus getup in a holiday 5K or shaving a mohawk into his hair to complete his Mr. T ensemble for a 1980s run ("Pity the fool!" he barked every time he passed someone), Dan absolutely committed to it. Sometimes this backfired. One year, he decided he would do Ironman Arizona in a Morphsuit, a spandex suit that covered every inch of his body, including his face.

"How are you going to see where you're going?" I asked when he told me of his plan the day before the race.

"I already tested it out, yo! It's see-through!" Dan effused. "It's legit!"

But on race day, Dan found that his costume was not so legit after all. A few miles into the 112-mile bike portion of the race, Dan realized that seeing out of the suit would not be a problem but getting food in would be.

"FRIENDS! COUNTRYMEN! LEND ME YOUR EARS!" he hollered as he rolled into the first aid station, stunning the volunteers into silence. They had seen lots of spandex on the course, but nothing quite like this. Dan pointed to his amorphous face. "I NEED A MOUTH HOLE!" When Dan and I crossed paths on the course later that day, he hollered through the jagged tear encircling his lips:

"YO! WHY DIDN'T YOU TALK ME OUT OF THIS?"

I could only shake my head and laugh.

Dan eventually moved to San Francisco, after falling in love with someone who lived there. The relationship turned out to be a dud, but Dan's love for the City by the Bay was the real deal.

You guys should come visit, Dan said just about every time we texted. There's this dope race you would love. It's pandemonium! Shenanigans! Tomfoolery!

While tomfoolery with Dan sounded entertaining, I didn't have time for that. I was too busy to fly out to San Francisco for a fun run.

That excuse went out the window the night I decided to embark on my year of running misadventures. If I had time to fly to Florida for a naked 5K, I certainly had time to go to San Francisco for a fun run with my friend. I filled out registrations for Dan, Neil, and myself and then forwarded the confirmation to Dan. He replied within seconds:

THIS IS GONNA BE SO MUCH FUN! WHICH ONE OF MY COS-TUMES SHOULD I WEAR? Even reading his email, I could hear his stoke blaring through the computer screen.

Bay to Breakers, the world's oldest footrace, is not your typical running event. Most of the time, saying that a race is steeped in history implies a certain level of decorum, with the designation of being "the world's oldest footrace" evoking a sense of tradition, honor, and dignity. Not so at Bay to Breakers. Tradition is everywhere, sure, but in highly unconventional ways. And instead of honor and dignity, there are gorilla suits and aid stations stocked with cupcakes and Jell-O shots.

The race didn't start out that way, though. When it was founded in 1912, it was a serious competition for elite runners only. After a devastating earthquake in 1906, which had destroyed over 80 percent of San Francisco, the city was searching for something to boost morale and give residents something to rally around. The San Francisco Cross-City Race was their solution: a footrace that started at the San Francisco Bay, blocks from the Embarcadero, and traveled west through the city to Ocean Beach, where breakers crash into the Pacific coast. Residents loved having a world-class competition in the streets of San Francisco, turning out in droves to cheer on the racers.

Over the years, neighborhood pride became a competition of its own, with each district trying to show bigger and better displays of support for racers along the course. As the friendly rivalry intensified, things started to get a little rowdy. It was fast becoming the biggest and best party of the year.

In the 1940s, revelry spilled off the sidelines and into the race itself when one competitor showed up dressed as a pirate. He finished in last place—a failure in elite racing but not in San Francisco, where unconventionality is celebrated. Captain Kidd became an icon. Each year, more and more people showed up to race in costume, transforming the event—eventually renamed Bay to Breakers—into a massive carnival for racers and spectators.

The crazy train was rolling, and San Francisco was having too much fun to try to stop it. In 1978, a group of track athletes from the University of California–Davis decided to enter the race as a centipede, tying 13 runners together to complete the race in tandem. Another icon was born, and since then, Centipedes have become their own unique category within the race, with teams showing up in matching costumes and bungee-cord belts to vie for top honors in tandem running.

A Centipede team was next to us in the starting corral the morning we did Bay to Breakers: a line of women dressed in identical green uniforms, each sporting the iconic crown and torch of the Statue of Liberty. On the other side of us was a man in a gorilla suit with his partner, who was wearing a banana costume. And in the middle, there was our throwback threesome, clad in retro running short-shorts and striped knee socks. Dan, true to form, had woken up early that morning to wield a blow-dryer for a perfectly feathered Farrah Fawcett 'do. I accessorized my high-waisted red shorts with oversized 1970s eyeglasses and pigtails. We were groovy.

The starting gun went off and everyone cheered. "Stay weird, San Francisco!" Dan hollered, the last syllable trailing off into a yodel. He flung another tortilla as we set off for shenanigans.

Stay weird, indeed. Though a competitive elite race still exists at Bay to Breakers, the majority of the runners sign up to let their freak flag fly. Bay to Breakers is an unofficial holiday in San Francisco; the city shuts down, and more than 125,000 residents decorate their front porches and set up unique aid stations for the runners. In the first miles of the race, we photobombed a live broadcast on a local news station, limbo-danced under an elaborate display, and stopped at a kissing booth staffed by puppies. And the aid stations only got better from there.

Then there were the costumes. Runners were a moving circus of superhero capes and neon-colored tutus, devil horns and leather chaps. There were Oompa Loompas, giant M&M's, Ghostbusters, Pac-Man characters, and Wookies. There were dozens of shark costumes and one runner who dressed as a *Baywatch* lifeguard, blowing his whistle and making a scene every time he saw a dorsal fin. Halfway through the course, a Centipede team dressed in salmon costumes bisected the field as they ran "upstream" from the finish line to the start. One man navigated the course on stilts. A few wore nothing at all, because at Bay to Breakers, anything (or in this case, nothing) goes.

The race passed through colorful neighborhoods, each with its own distinct personality and pride. Although the race itself is all but unrecognizable from the elite intention of its founders, one thing remains: Bay to Breakers is undeniably a showcase of San Francisco. The unconventional, the peculiar, and the unusual thrive in this city, where people are free to embrace oddity. As I ran, it occurred to me that Bay to Breakers is not so much a race as it is a 7-mile love letter to San Francisco. This was clear as Dan became our impromptu tour guide during the race, pointing out the landmarks of each neighborhood and the places he loved the most. Dan was, in a word, stoked.

"HEYOOOOO!" Dan howled whenever he saw something that thrilled him, whether it was an impressive costume, a funny spectator sign, or just someone who had really good running form. Even though the course was 7 miles, he was easily doubling that distance as he crisscrossed the road, doling out high fives and fist bumps.

I had forgotten how fun it was to run with him. That's the thing about people like Dan. He never seems to lose his affection for running. In addition to his years-long streak of running at least a mile each day, Dan has entered just about every race he can. And throughout all of it, I have never once heard him talk about being burned out or disillusioned; he seems happy just to go outside and have a good time. His stoke levels are always high, and the best part about it? It's contagious.

As runners, we sometimes focus on the parts of the sport that are difficult and gritty. We buy into the delusion that success comes when we suffer and that misery is the price to pay for going farther or becoming faster. That all-or-nothing mentality can become all-consuming, as we begin to see each run in terms of success or failure. There is no in-between—and certainly no room for fun.

But Dan is proof that running doesn't have to be so serious. And races like Bay to Breakers remind us that at the end of the day, we're all just a bunch of idiots, gallivanting about in spandex. Why not have some fun with it?

Don't get me wrong. It's good to work hard and set ambitious goals. But it's also good to put on a goofy costume and eat midrace cupcakes. And now that I've done just that, I think it should be mandatory every year—a prophylactic dose of stoke to ward off burnout.

In the final stretch of Bay to Breakers, as we rolled over the hills of Golden Gate Park, I glanced over at Dan and Neil, who were running alongside me. Dan's fanny pack was bouncing all over the place, and Neil's orange wig was crooked. Both of them had serious wedgies from their short-shorts. But the big, goofy smiles on their faces said it all. I let out a whoop as we turned a corner and headed for the final stretch along Ocean Beach. The morning of shenanigans was exactly what I needed.

"All right, knuckleheads," Dan said, his tone suddenly serious. "We've got to plan for the next one. I'm going to text you guys some ideas for costumes after I go through my closet tonight."

Neil and I looked at each other and laughed. Of course we'd be back. "Just promise me no jorts," Neil replied.

Dan skipped toward the finish chute, feathered hair fluttering in the wind.

"The only thing I can promise is THIS IS GONNA BE SO MUCH FUN!"

14

AND JILL CAME
TUMBLING AFTER

LIKE MANY AMERICANS, I had built up a dignified image of England over the years, flush with royalty, posh accents, and afternoon tea with crumpets. The hills would be green and rolling; the countryside, dotted with quaint cottages. The ladies and gentlemen—and they could only be ladies and gentlemen, of course—would be impeccably dressed and overwhelmingly polite.

Nowhere in my image was there a boisterous fellow named Mango. I certainly didn't envision Mango in little more than a "budgy smuggler." And I definitely didn't expect to see the scantily clad Mango bounce, arse-over-teakettle, down a hill.

Then again, nothing about this trip was what I had expected.

I suppose I should have done more research on the Cooper's Hill Cheese Roll. The event crossed my desk every year, usually in the form of an email from a colleague that read: Get a load of this. A round of jokes would ensue, usually some variation of That sounds gouda and You chedda brie-lieve it. A funny little race in England sounded like a refreshing departure in a sport where athletes sometimes take themselves a little too seriously.

And now I had a chance to actually participate. The premise of the race sounded simple enough: chase an 8-pound wheel of dairy down an incline. I ate cheese all the time. I ran down hills all the time. How hard could this be? I made myself a cheese plate and nibbled away as I booked my flight to England, confident that this was one race I was going to nail.

The closer the race got, the more excited I became. I practiced for it by running a grassy downhill at a playground near my house, and it was fun. The concept of chasing a wheel of cheese down a hill was so bizarre, I couldn't help but giggle my way through every training session. After all, I was preparing to chase after a dairy product! This was going to be the best race ever.

"I grew up in Wisconsin," I'd say with a laugh, as I told people about my race plans. "Technically, I've been training my whole life for this." When the customs agent at Heathrow scanned my passport and asked what brought me to London, I smiled coyly and said, "I'm chasing a wheel of cheese down a hill." And when

I checked into my hotel in the Gloucestershire countryside, I asked how far of a walk it was to Cooper's Hill.

"Cooper's Hill?" asked the front-desk clerk with an amused smirk. "You're here to watch tomorrow?"

"I'm here to chase the cheese," I said confidently.

His face quickly morphed from warm hospitality to grave concern. "Do you know what you're doing?"

I stammered uncomfortably. Was he messing with me? He had to be messing with me.

"Charlie!" He yelled across the lobby to the hotel bar, where a lone bartender was polishing the wood top. "This lady says she's doing the cheese roll!"

Charlie looked up from his bar rag, glanced at me, and snorted. "You know what you're doing?"

"Why are you asking me that?" I replied, smiling, trying not to reveal my slowly building panic.

Charlie snorted again and went back to polishing the bar, but not before announcing, "She doesn't know what she's doing."

I looked back and forth at the two men, confused. What could be so complicated about running down a hill?

"Look," said the front-desk clerk. "I'm finished here in an hour. Meet me at the bar, and we'll tell you everything you need to know."

As it turned out, what I needed to know was that I knew absolutely nothing about cheese rolling. Before I even sat down at the bar, my new friend Trevor, the front-desk clerk, had cued up a photo on his phone from a previous year's event. It wasn't a photo of a race, a wheel of cheese, or even the hill itself. It was a foot, facing the exact opposite direction a foot should face on the body.

"Is that . . . ?" I gasped.

"It is," Trevor replied, clearly proud to have evoked in me a perfect mixture of shock and disgust. I didn't even know a foot could bend like that.

"Holy shit," I whispered.

Charlie snorted again. They were right: I didn't know what I was doing. My crash course in cheese rolling was to begin immediately.

No one is entirely sure how the annual Cooper's Hill Cheese Roll came about, only that it's been around for about as long as Cooper's Hill itself. The landmark, which is located just outside the town of Brockworth in Gloucestershire, is not a quaint, grassy incline. Rather, it's a steep, gnarled beast of terrain, rising 650 feet at a 50 percent grade. Half of the hill is covered in bumps, and the other half, in deep divots. All of it is covered in mud. Overgrown grasses and shrubs make it difficult to ascertain just where you'll be stepping.

"But it doesn't matter," Trevor said, waving his hand dismissively as he showed me photos of the hill. "You're falling too fast to control where you're going, anyway." He should know—that photo on his phone is of his foot. He's not sure whether it was a bump or a divot that broke his ankle, only that "it fucking hurt."

"So, you're retired from cheese rolling?" I asked.

Charlie, who was listening to our conversation as he pulled pints of beer from the tap, snorted again. Trevor smiled.

"Are you kidding?" asked Trevor. "And miss the fun?"

The next morning, I met Trevor and Charlie in the hotel parking lot, along with several of their friends. Although the cheese didn't roll until noon, they told me we needed to head over there at 9:00 in the morning. As the event's reputation grew each year, so too did the crowds; finding a spot to watch the race meant getting there as early as possible. But hours before the event, the crowd was already six deep along the course, leaning into the steep hill like a fun-house mirror.

Trevor grabbed my arm and began pushing through the wall of people. "Come with me. I'll get you inside."

"Inside" meant to the base of the hill, where a wall of hay bales formed a de facto finish line for the cheese roll. It was there that I met Sarah, a chain-smoking ball of sass wearing mud-encrusted galoshes. Trevor introduced her as the organizer but was quickly shushed.

"No one is in charge here," Sarah whispered with a glare. "We're just having fun. Yes?"

"Right," said Trevor, taking the hint. "Yes."

As it turns out, the organizational structure of the Cooper's Hill Cheese Roll resembles a game of Hot Potato. In 2009, Gloucestershire police cracked down on the event, saying it was too dangerous and a drain on local resources. That year, more than 15,000 people had packed into the countryside surrounding Cooper's Hill, overloading police forces and block-ing traffic in the rural community. Deep crowds made it hard for ambulances to reach injured competitors, of which there were many. Spectators slipped in the mud, got drunk, and occasion-ally started fights. It was an undignified embarrassment to the town, they said, and it needed to be stopped.

And it did stop—for one year. But then, quietly, the cheese made its way back to the top of the hill in 2011. The police warned that anyone associated with the cheese roll would be held liable for any injury or issues that arose from the event, so an unspoken agreement was made with the town: No one was officially affiliated with the event. When local cheese makers were threatened with legal consequences for providing wheels of Gloucester for the event, someone anonymously donated wheels of foam "cheese" that technically didn't belong to any-one. Bales of hay spontaneously appeared at the base of the hill every year. And instead of an organized race, with liability waiv-ers and legal responsibility, anyone who wanted to enter the race could simply walk up to the start line on the top of the hill. No names, no forms, no questions asked. There is no official website with information on the race, yet people from all over the world know to show up at Cooper's Hill at noon on the third Monday in May. The date and time never change. Google Maps makes Cooper's Hill easy to find, and if not, a local will point you in the right direction. Most locals are heading there them-selves; they would be happy to give you a lift.

There are signs posted all over the hill that warn participants and spectators of the potential for danger at such an
event. Apparently, a rolling wheel of cheese can reach speeds of
70 miles per hour (who knew?), and if it misses the bales of hay
at the bottom, it's on the spectators to duck out of the way in
time. If you go to the top of the hill, it's your responsibility to get
to the bottom. If you hurt yourself, there are no ambulances on
the hill waiting to shuttle you to the hospital. This event is, as
the signs declare repeatedly and in bold print, **ENTIRELY AT YOUR
OWN RISK.**

So who's in charge of the Cooper's Hill Cheese Roll? No one.
And everyone. Though the event isn't formally organized by anyone, somehow everyone who needs to be there shows up: Medics go for a stroll with their bags of supplies and stop by to watch
(and hope their services aren't needed). A few locals with mega-
phones remind people to keep an eye out for flying cheese. And
the local rugby team shows up to practice at the base of the hill.

"Wait, the rugby team is practicing here?" I asked, as Sarah
pointed out the men in black-and-white uniforms. "I don't get it."

"You will soon," Trevor replied. By now, I knew better than
to question it. I also knew better than to question where he got
his pre-race fuel while I was talking to Sarah: a can of Heineken
beer in one hand and a can of Thatchers Gold Cider in the other.

"The men start in 20 minutes. Are you heading up?" Sarah
asked him. Trevor chugged the beer and crushed the can before
starting in on the cider.

"Yeah," he belched as he turned to climb up the hill. "I'll give it a go."

This is the general attitude of cheese rollers. The hundred or so men and women who race every year aren't hard-core athletes. Some, like the defending champion (a local named Chris), are competitive and train to win. (Cash prize? No. But the winner does get to keep the cheese.) But for most of the competitors, it's a lark. That's certainly the case for Mango, a lanky Australian wearing nothing but a bikini bottom, or "budgy smuggler," and a pair of boots.

"It's the best!" Mango buzzes excitedly, adjusting his skimpy bottoms before heading to the start line. "I can't wait." I can't tell if his exuberance is fueled by adrenaline or something chemical— maybe both. Mango, who lives in London, drove out to Cooper's Hill to watch the race last year and ended up entering on a whim. He called it the most thrilling thing he'd ever done. He also found it to be the most painful thing—for weeks, his scrapes and bruises served as both a reminder of his stupidity and a badge of honor. He proudly points out his scars from the previous year's race.

"So why do the race in . . . whatever this is?" I point at the budgy smuggler.

"Why not?" Mango cackles. "I'm going to get torn up anyway." He raises his arms in the air and lets out a loud whoop. The crowd responds in kind. Everyone loves Mango, if only for the added layer of absurdity on an already ridiculous event.

At 11:55 a.m., the Cheesemaster, a man in a top hat who goes by the name Jem, takes the microphone and reminds everyone to watch out for flying cheese. The crowd roars as last call for the men's competitive wave takes place. If you want to race, get to the top of the hill. If you're not sure, there will be other waves to join. And if going down doesn't sound appealing, there's also a race up the hill—much slower and cheeseless, Jem tells the crowd, but just as fun.

There's a countdown and then the ceremonial launching of the cheese. The disc, a white wheel the size of a basketball, barrels down the incline, picking up speed as it bounces off the rocks along the way. Also bouncing off the rocks: 20 gentlemen, including Trevor and Mango.

There's no way to describe the cheese roll other than to say it's carnage. Within seconds, the men go from running to tumbling, legs and arms akimbo as they bounce down the hill. Occasionally, one will find himself upright for a few steps, only to catch a foot on a rock and cartwheel again. The crowd winces and groans in vicarious pain. As the competitors plummet to the finish line, the members of the rugby team, moving in unison, plant their feet in the mud and crouch down low. No one hits a hay bale—instead, they launch into a brick wall of strapping young men.

"See?" Sarah points matter-of-factly. "Practice." Apparently, getting roughed up by a bevy of tumbling cheese chasers is excellent training for the rugby scrum.

The winner, Chris, a lean 30-year-old in worn jeans, a colorful shirt, and a buzz cut, has defended his title. In all, he's won 21 cheese-rolling crowns, making him a hot commodity for local businesses, whose logos emblazon his sponsored shirt to create a tumbling, muddy billboard. He believes he has torn his left calf muscle, though he doesn't seek medical treatment. Apparently, he's gotten off easy this year—in past races, he's sustained a broken ankle, concussions, and kidney damage. Chris directs the medics to several other men crumpled on the ground. Mango is among them. He, too, eschews medical help, sitting up, then standing, then shaking his head as if his brain is an Etch A Sketch that needs clearing.

"Whooo!" Mango raises his arms in victory, revealing a body tattooed by mud and blood. The crowd goes wild. He high-fives the other competitors, including Trevor, who somehow has made it to the bottom in one (very muddy but largely unscathed) piece.

I'm strongly reconsidering doing this race. Someone reassures me that the competitive wave is much riskier than the casual "fun" waves yet to come, but I can't help but think about what Charlie and Trevor told me the night before: The women's cheese rolls typically have more injuries than the men's.

"Why is that?" I asked.

"Girls don't know how to fall" is Charlie's explanation. "Boys grew up fighting, playing rugby, getting dirty. We know how to take a hit. Do you?"

"I think so," I said, recalling the many times I'd tripped and skinned my knee while trail running. In training and racing, I had proven that I had a high pain threshold. In fact, I had always thought of myself as a tough cookie. Charlie and Trevor looked at each other with raised eyebrows. They didn't say it, but I knew what they were thinking: *She doesn't know what she's doing.*

That evening, my crash course in cheese rolling also included a crash course in falling. If I felt myself losing my footing, they instructed, I should try to fall backward into the hill, not forward. Try to land on my bum instead of putting my hands behind me. And if I lost control, I should go limp. "Don't tense up," Trevor warned. "It only makes things worse."

At the time, I thought they were preparing me for the unlikely event I might take a tumble. Now, at the foot of Cooper's Hill, watching wave after wave of mayhem, I was beginning to see that falling was an absolute inevitability.

I tried to talk myself into doing the cheese roll. I tried to talk myself out of doing the cheese roll. I tried to do something other than freak out behind a bale of hay: *Fuck. Fuck, fuck, fuckity fuck fuck fuck.*

Finally, I made a compromise with myself: I would go down the hill but not competitively. I'd stick to the side of the course, go slowly, and slide down on my ass if necessary.

As it turned out, several other women had the same plan. While the men were perfectly happy to fling themselves down the hill, the women took a more sensible approach to the cheese roll—namely, one that wouldn't end in a neck brace. As our wave congregated at the top of the hill, the women organized into two groups: a small-but-competitive group, which included last year's winner, and the rest of us bucket-listers who were perfectly okay with giving up our right to dairy victory.

Cheesemaster Jem counted down from 10 and then bowled the wheel down the hill. The competitive women barreled down after it, throwing elbows and shoving each other out of the way. As they landed at the base with concussions and dislocated shoulders, the rest of us held hands and carefully sidestepped down the incline. One by one, we slipped on the mud, squealing as we skidded down the hill. Our rear ends awkwardly and painfully bumped over rocks and divots, yet we couldn't stop laughing. At the base of the hill, we slid to the feet of the rugby players, who gamely scooped us up and carried us over their shoulders to safety behind the bales of hay, revealing our torn-up backsides to the cheering spectators.

Did I cop out? Absolutely. Joining an ass-sledding flotilla of women wasn't what I had set out to do. But remember, I originally came to England to drink afternoon tea and jog down a gentle grassy incline. Instead, I got my new friends Trevor and Charlie, double-fisting morning beers and teaching me how to fall. I came for a silly run and would leave with a scar on my butt cheek and the craziest story to explain it. There was no race medal or T-shirt, but as far as souvenirs went, this was a pretty good one.

When I got back to my hotel that afternoon, I threw away my torn, muddy shorts and soaked my bruised rear end in the bathtub. My phone buzzed with a text from Neil.

How was the cheese chasing? Neil asked. Was it everything you dreamed it would be?

Hell, no. I replied. Nothing at all like I expected.

No?

No. It was even better.

ALL THE FALLS

Runners don't fall.

Yes, a runner may arrive home from a workout with a skinned knee. That happens all the time. Ditto for muddy butts and bruises in strange places. But when you point at these battle scars and ask a runner what happened, the words "I fell" will never be uttered. It's a quirk of runner lingo—they may "take a digger" or "have a yard sale," but runners never, ever fall.

Over the years, I've heard runners describe their falls in the most colorful ways. My favorites:

plummeted

visited **DIRT CITY**

KISSED *the* **PAVEMENT**

COLLECTED A SOUVENIR

WENT *headlong*

Spilled

Played whack-a-mole

went down

KEELED OVER

EVEL-KNIEVELED

TOPPLED

Bombed

Went ASS OVER tea-kettle

ATE DIRT

Donated BLOOD

PLAYED **ScarWars**

HIT THE SMELLING SALTS ✳

GAVE THE TRAIL A HUG

TESTED THE LAW OF GRAVITY

Slipped

HELD DOWN *the* **CONCRETE**

Flew first class *on* **AIR FACE-PLANT**

BIT *the* **DUST**

ATTACKED *an* ANTHILL

TUMBLED

MOWED THE GRASS WITH MY FACE

GOT A MUD FACIAL

flattened *the* mountain

TESTED MY ASS CUSHIONING

TOOK A FLYING LESSON

HIT THE DECK

MADE AN EMERGENCY LANDING

THANK HELL
FOR LITTLE GIRLS

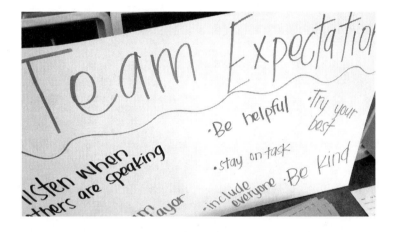

OF ALL THE THINGS I SIGNED UP FOR in my year of discomfort, running with a gaggle of 10-year-old girls scared me the most.

I'm just going to come right out and say it: I don't really enjoy kids. Don't get me wrong—I can muster up a convincing display of excitement when my friends announce a pregnancy, because I'm genuinely excited that *they* are excited. And I can smile and make goo-goo noises at an infant for a few minutes. When a toddler is doing toddlerish things, I will definitely pretend like it is charming and adorable, and I will dutifully click "like" on the obligatory first-day-of-school photos posted on social media. If you are a blood relative and/or have information that could implicate me in a federal crime, I will even babysit for your children.

But the only thing I actually like about hanging out with kids is the part when they leave.

It's not their fault. The kids are fine; I'm sure they're great, even. I'm the one with the problem. Even when I was a kid, I had a hard time being around other kids. As a deaf student in a public school, I was a pretty easy target for bullying. In addition to reading, writing, and arithmetic, my elementary years taught me that children can be intensely cruel. If kids weren't making fun of my accent, they'd be standing behind me and yelling my name, knowing full well I'd be oblivious to what was taking place. And then there were the really mean ones—the ones who would taunt me on the playground, calling me names and warning fellow students not to sit or play with me.

Despite my best efforts in adulthood to see children as the little angels their parents think they are, my hackles rise the second anyone under the age of 12 enters the room. Maybe it's not that I don't like kids. Perhaps a more accurate way of putting it is that kids full-on terrify me. And based on the number of tykes who hide behind their mother's legs when they meet me, I'd say the feeling's mutual.

So, when the local chapter of Girls on the Run said they were looking for volunteers to help out at their weeklong summer camp, I clenched my teeth and pulled from the well of feigned enthusiasm typically reserved for my friends' pregnancy announcements: "Oh, yay! That sounds like so much fun!"

My experience with Girls on the Run was, to that point, limited to a brief interview with a program representative for an article I was writing. The premise of it sounded great—a youth development program that uses running as a platform to inspire girls to be joyful, healthy, and confident. I could definitely get behind that notion. After all, I know firsthand how the sport can open doors and inspire limitless potential. I also love the program's kick-ass ethos:

> We believe every girl can embrace who she is,
> can define who she wants to be,
> can rise to any challenge,
> can change the world.

It is an important, powerful, profound lesson for young girls, and I commented as much during the interview. I guess I shouldn't have done that, because the representative cocked her head to the side and smiled: "Why don't you come help teach it?"

No. Nope. Nonononononononono.

"Sure," I smiled. "I'd *love* to."

And just like that, the following week, I was sitting crisscross applesauce in a circle of third graders. The lead coach, a perky college student named Brooklyn, spoke to the group with wide-eyed enthusiasm.

"This week is going to be really fun, you guys!" Coach Brooklyn said animatedly, gesticulating wildly as she spoke. "We're going to make so many new friends!" I suppressed a reflexive urge to roll my eyes.

As Brooklyn laid out the instructions for the first activity—a getting-to-know-you game—a sharp finger poked me in the ribs. I turned to my left, where a young girl with a round face and curly red hair was looking up at me.

"What's that in your ear?" she whispered, pointing at my hearing aid. My face flushed as I had flashbacks to elementary school. This is how it always started.

"It's a hearing aid," I said quietly. I put my finger to my lips: "Shhh, pay attention to Coach Brooklyn."

But she was undeterred. The girl shifted into a crouching position, leaning in for a closer look at my ear. I could feel her breath on my neck, and then:

"CAN YOU HEAR ME?" she screeched. In unison, every face in the room snapped to us. I cringed, trying to decide if I should run out of the room or break out my headlock skills.

"Olivia," Brooklyn chastised, her face scrunching into an exaggerated frown. "That's not very nice."

The group turned back to the activity at hand—thank goodness for the short attention spans of children—and I mentally vowed to stay in the background. The less I interacted with these kids, the better.

At Camp Girls on the Run, the theme of the week was "Emotions." All activities would be centered around building a bigger emotional vocabulary and learning how to better recognize and express those emotions in healthy, constructive ways.

"Let's talk about anger!" Coach Brooklyn said in one of the first lessons of the camp. "What are things that can make us angry?" The girls piled on with responses, ranging from annoying siblings to friends who cheat at board games.

"So, if all of these make us angry, do we always react in the same way?"

"No!" the girls chimed in unison, kicking off a discussion about the many forms of anger, from irked to irate.

"Mad!" shouted one girl when Brooklyn asked for the different names we use for the emotion. "Frustrated!" another chimed in. The voices of two dozen girls overlapped: "Upset!" "Annoyed!" "Fuming!" "Crabby!"

"Pissed off!" came a voice from the back of the room. Everyone gasped, unsure of how to respond. In conservative Utah, where people shout "Oh, my heck!" when they slam their finger in the cupboard and claim that a hard workout "really kicked my trash," saying "pissed" was akin to an f-bomb.

"Who said that?" Coach Brooklyn asked. Everyone turned to locate the source. And there was Olivia, pushing a tangle of red curls off her forehead and grinning proudly, exposing a mouth full of braces. I covered my mouth, trying to suppress my snort-laugh. I liked this kid's style. I had gotten her all wrong. She wasn't a mean girl—just a loud one.

Throughout the week, the girls participated in activities that used running as a teaching tool. Sometimes those tools took the form of a prompt given to the campers ("Talk about a time when you felt happy"), which they would then discuss as they ran together in pairs. Other times, it was a more structured lesson. In one activity, campers ran laps at various effort levels before responding to a hypothetical scenario to simulate how the physiological effects of emotions can lead to rash responses. (The lesson: Take a breather to collect your thoughts before you say or do something you'll regret.) In another activity, the girls played "Emotion Detective," where partners sprinted to various coaches stationed around the field to collect a card with an emotion listed. One girl would give clues in the form of facial expressions and body language, and the other would try to identify the sentiment being conveyed.

"You're scared!" Olivia shouted to her partner, Morgan, who was glaring with wide eyes and a puckered mouth. Morgan shook her head and puckered her lips even more and then extended her arms into the air, high above her head.

"You're amazed!"

Morgan shook her head again and wiggled her outstretched fingers.

"Surprised? Excited? You feel like kissing me?"

Morgan's eyes bulged so much, I thought they might explode.

"Oh! I know!" Olivia hopped excitedly, her voice now a shout. "YOU FEEL LIKE POOPING!"

"Olivia!" Coach Brooklyn scolded from across the field. I hid my face behind my stack of cards until the giggles went away.

The other coaches handled the kids expertly. I admired their ability to converse with the girls at their level—it came so naturally to them. I never quite made it to that level. The few times I attempted a conversation with a camper, it didn't go well. In one case, a girl named Summit responded to my attempt at making small talk during snack time with a look of confusion and a blunt question: "Are you *really* a coach?" The rest of the girls at the table laughed.

So, yeah, I'm about as popular with 10-year-olds today as I was when I was actually 10 years old. But that's okay. Going to running camp with these girls helped me realize that kids really are fine. Great, even. I could probably cut them some slack.

Contrary to what I believed, kids do possess the capacity to be kind, empathetic, wonderful humans—they just need the time and opportunity to flex that muscle. Being around girls reminded me of what it was like to be that age—and of what came after. Soon, these girls will discover that the learning curve for humanity is steep and slippery and strewn with complications. Their bodies will change in strange and confusing ways. Their best friends will become strangers in the ever-shifting alliances of middle school. They'll fall in love and get their hearts broken and mended a time or three. They will say the wrong thing and lose someone or something they care about deeply, or maybe they'll say the exact right thing and change someone's world. They will think they know what it is to be happy or sad, and then life will take an unexpected turn, and they will learn a whole new depth of feeling. They'll experience all the emotions they discussed at camp—and then some. It will be wonderful, except for the parts that are just so excruciatingly awful.

When those moments happen, as they inevitably will, I want these girls to feel strong, to understand that mishaps are not setbacks, and that fear is not necessarily something to be afraid of. What seems scary at first glance could really be wonder or joy in a visage you just don't recognize. Or maybe Olivia's right about the pooping thing—I don't know.

The good news is that if they're not sure, they do know one thing is for certain: A run with a friend is a pretty good way to figure it out.

16

GET OFF MY BACK

ON THE MANTEL IN MY HOME, you'll find a tidy assortment of glass and bronze figurines—awards accumulated at races over the years. Only one of them—my recent addition from the naked 5K in Florida—is mine. The rest belong to my prize stallion of a husband.

Neil has always been the speedy one in our household, making quick work of even the toughest courses, while I'm more inclined to awkwardly bumble through a race. Luckily, in races we do together, I at least manage to finish before the awards ceremony, where I can settle into a role where I really excel: the proud, sweaty partner, snapping photos and *woo-hooing* as Neil takes his spot on the podium.

I've long joked that the only way I could ever win a race is by riding piggyback on Neil. But at the annual Midwest Wife Carrying Championship in Frederick, South Dakota, it wasn't a joke. I could literally ride my horsey—er, husband—to a win.

But first, I had to convince the horsey.

"No," Neil groaned when I told him about the race. "No way." Though he was used to being roped into my ridiculous plans, this one was simply too much. Besides, hadn't he already done enough for me this year? After all, he had driven a crew vehicle through a dust storm during my 50-mile race, carried a coffin through a muddy obstacle course while wearing spandex, and donned a pair of chafing, bun-hugging jorts at Bay to Breakers. He was done.

"But . . . ," I started my wheedling.

"Nope," he replied firmly, standing up to walk away from the conversation. "Find another pony. This one's out to pasture."

I knew I had only one chance to get him on board. I would have to choose my words carefully. I took a deep breath and blurted out: "The winner takes home his wife's weight in beer!"

Neil stopped mid-stride and cocked his head. "Really?"

"It's the official award of wife-carrying championships."

He paused and then nodded his head. "All right," he said, "but after this one, I'm done."

"Sure," I nodded, as Neil left the room with a neigh.

If wife carrying sounds like a made-up sport, that's because technically it is. No one really knows how the sport originated. Some say it's based on a 19th-century practice of Finnish men, who would court women by running into their villages, picking them up, and carrying them off. But there's no evidence such a custom actually existed—and besides, as most women will tell you, abduction is not so much a seduction tool as it is a guaranteed way to get kicked in the testicles.

A more probable origin story lies in the same time frame, when an infamous thief named Herkko Rosvo-Ronkainen led a team of bandits on a crime spree through the villages of Finland, where they'd steal essential supplies like food and ale. Occasionally, they'd kidnap someone's wife, carrying her out into the forest in the dead of night. No matter which origin story you believe, the moral is that being a woman in 19th-century Finland really sucked.

Somewhere along the way, wife carrying evolved from a disturbingly chauvinistic practice to a wacky competition. Today, thousands of couples race at regional championships each year in hopes of securing a spot at the World Eukonkanto (Finnish for "wife carry") Championships. The annual Finn Fest in Frederick, South Dakota, is one such regional qualifier. In addition to winning the wife's weight in beer, the top couple wins $500 toward their entry and travel costs for the North American Wife Carrying Championship in Newry, Maine, and—if they rise to the top in that race—on to Finland.

The possibility of traveling to Maine and Finland sounded cool, but what Neil really wanted was the beer. While telling some friends about our upcoming wife-carrying race, someone asked how much beer we'd take home should we win. Neil excitedly did some math on a cocktail napkin. His eyes opened wide as he carried the two and came up with the final equation: "That's, like, an entire year's worth of beer!"

I peered at the numbers and smacked Neil in the stomach in mock rage. "Hey!" I said. "I don't weigh *that* much!"

The jokes and smack talk continued every time we told someone about the upcoming race. Unfortunately, however, the actual preparation never took place. Between our asynchronous work schedules—he on night shift, me on days—and a calendar full of other races, we just didn't have the time. On our rare days together, I'd jokingly mention what the Midwest Wife Carrying Championship website claimed: It is possible to train for the wife carrying competition everywhere in the middle of the daily routines: in the bath, in the super market, in the playground or in the body building center. Neil would laugh, and then we'd move on to something else.

So, the day before the race, while road-tripping from Utah to South Dakota, we decided we should probably give this carrying thing a whirl and figure out some kind of strategy. That night, after checking in to our hotel in Aberdeen, Neil opened his laptop and pulled up the website for the race. "The rules of wife carrying are as such," he read, in a deep, authoritative voice, tinged with what I believed to be an attempt at a Finnish accent:

1. The length of the official track is 277 yards.
2. The track must have sand, forested terrain, two log obstacles, and one water obstacle.
3. The wife may be your own, or your neighbor's, or you may find one further afield; however, she must be at least 17 years of age.
4. The wife must weigh more than 108 pounds. If she falls under this weight, she must wear a rucksack with added weight.
5. Each contestant takes care of his or her own safety and, if deemed necessary, insurance.

He closed his laptop.

"Sounds easy enough," said Neil. "I suppose we should practice now, huh?"

"Whoa, whoa, wait a second," I said. "What's with the insurance rule?"

"That's in case I drop you," Neil said, lowering to a crouch and patting his hindquarters. "Now, hop on!"

Our crash course in wife carrying took place inside our hotel room and out in the hallway. The first attempt was a flop. Piggyback riding was just not something we typically did together or, to be more precise, had *ever* done together.

I climbed on and held him tightly around his neck but slid down with every bounce of Neil's stride. The neck squeeze wasn't ideal for his breathing ability, either. We tried again, but this time I locked my ankles around Neil's waist. Another flop, giving me a cramp and restricting Neil's movement.

"All right," Neil sighed as he dropped me on the hotel bed. "Looks like we're going to have to do this Estonian style."

"Say what?"

Neil opened his laptop, typed in a few words, and then turned the screen to me. "Estonian style," I learned, was how the truly competitive teams did it: The wife hangs upside down on her husband's back, with her legs around his neck and her arms around his waist.

"No way!" I scoffed. "My face will be in your butt!"

"Should've thought of that before you got us into this, babe," Neil smiled at his serendipitous revenge. "Good thing I had bean burritos for lunch."

Neil turned around, and I awkwardly maneuvered into an unsteady handstand position. He hoisted my legs over his shoulders and stood up with a soft grunt. It was immediately clear our third attempt at wife carrying was also going to be a flop. This time it wasn't because the carry was ineffective—it actually worked shockingly well—but because we both were laughing so hard, we couldn't breathe.

A guest in a neighboring hotel room, upon hearing the clamor in the hallway, opened his door to see what was going on. The look of surprise on his face, followed by the hasty closing of the door, made us laugh even harder. Neil scurried into our room, with me still clinging to his back, and we fell over onto the bed, both of us hyperventilating with hilarity.

"This is so silly," I giggled, when I finally caught my breath. Neil turned to me, first with a smile and then a serious squint.

"No silliness tomorrow," Neil said. "We came to win."

The Midwest Wife Carrying Championship takes place as part of the annual Finn Fest in Frederick, South Dakota. Frederick is a tiny town—so tiny that the elementary, middle, and high schools are all housed in the same building. Main Street is only two blocks long, which makes the Finn Fest parade not that much different from what residents do every day, which is drive down the street waving at each other. It's the kind of small Midwestern town where everyone knows everyone, which also means everyone knows when they don't know someone. I discovered this when I entered the school building to use the restroom facilities. While on my way out of the building, someone stepped in my path and put a hand out to stop me.

"You're not from here, are you?" a short blonde woman said with concern.

"No, I live in Utah."

"Welcome!" she cried, extending her arms in the air to bring me in for a hug. "I'm Krysti!"

Within seconds, she was insisting on meeting Neil and on walking us down to the park where Finn Fest was being held and on introducing us to each one of the three dozen people who had come to Finn Fest.

"I thought this was supposed to be some big-deal championship race," Neil muttered under his breath.

"I did, too," I hissed.

"So where is it?" he wondered.

"Neil! Susan!" Krysti called from a park pavilion. "Come over here! I want you to meet Donna!"

Donna, it turned out, was a kind-faced grandmother who had been organizing the Finn Fest wife-carrying race since its inception in 2008. She was particularly excited for the 2018 edition, as it was the first year the race would serve as the Midwest championship. To mark the occasion, she had commissioned a special piece of artwork from a local artist—her daughter—for a winner's trophy. Donna excitedly pulled a box from underneath the picnic table and opened the lid.

"Go ahead!" she said, gesturing for us to come closer. "Take a look!"

Upon a carved wooden platform stood a plastic Ken doll. Attached to his shoulders, in an Estonian-style hold, was Barbie. Both plastic bodies had been spray-painted gold. It was the ultimate in kitsch and ridiculousness, and I had never wanted something on my mantel so badly in my life. I looked up at Neil with determination.

"We *have* to win," I said. I would accept nothing else. "If you don't run fast, I'm going to take you out back and shoot you."

Neil replied with a neigh.

To win the Midwest Wife Carrying Championship, Donna explained, we would have to beat out eight other couples, including the three-time reigning champions, the Nickelsons.

"They're quite good at it," Donna said, pointing out a couple at the lemonade stand. "Very speedy. I think it's because Don has a low center of gravity. He doesn't topple over on the obstacles as easily."

In other words, Don was short. This didn't bode well for Neil, who stands at 6 feet, 5 inches. Donna patted Neil on the arm reassuringly. "Don't worry. I'm sure you'll do great!"

As it turned out, the Nickelsons weren't our only serious adversaries. It seemed that several couples had been training for the race all year, hoping to unseat the Nickelsons and win that trip to Maine. The competition Neil and I had treated as a lark was serious business here in Frederick. But there was no time to fret about that now, as Donna announced it was time for the race to begin.

The tiny crowd shifted its attention from the rubber-boot-tossing competition (another perplexing Finnish sport) to the 200-plus-yard wife-carrying course. Donna explained the course over the loudspeaker: It winded over a series of logs, around a pole, and under three parallel dowels, each one set at a lower height than the preceding one. The water hazard, she explained, would not be on the course this year (apparently, the inflatable kiddie pool they normally used had sprung a leak).

"Who wants to go first?" Donna asked, clapping her hands and turning to the competitors. We, the competitors, stared each other down in silence.

"We'll do it," said the Nickelsons at last, with a steely gaze.

"Ladies and gentlemen!" Donna boomed over the loudspeaker. "Your defending champions, the Nickelsons!" The crowd hooted for their hometown heroes.

The couple marched over to the picnic table that marked the start line, where Mrs. Nickelson climbed onto her husband's shoulders, Estonian-style, with ease.

"On your mark . . . get set . . . ," Donna inhaled deeply to build suspense. "Go!"

The Nickelsons sprang into action. Mr. Nickelson hopped over the logs and sprinted under the poles without flinching. I admired their form—Mrs. Nickelson was affixed securely to her husband, whose running form seemed unencumbered by the woman on his back. I grimaced at Neil. Perhaps we should have practiced more.

More couples went through the course, each one accompanied by loud cheers from the spectators, but none looked as slick as the Nickelsons. Finally, it was our turn.

"Who's next?" Donna crooned, looking at us expectantly. We were the only couple who hadn't raced yet.

"I guess we are?" Neil said hesitantly as he took my hand and led me to the picnic table. The crowd cheered warmly when Donna announced we had traveled all the way from Utah.

This was it. This was for the trophy. For Neil's beer. It was the big show. I mounted my horsey, Estonian-style. "On your mark," Donna sang. "Get set . . . go!"

Neil took off in a sprint, while I held on for dear life. And then, suddenly, he stopped. Then stepped over a limb. Then stopped again and stepped over another limb.

"Are you serious?" I said, unhooking one arm to spank Neil on the butt. Now was not the time to be careful. "Run!" He barreled under the parallel bars, my feet brushing the poles. The crowd laughed and cheered as Neil sprinted across the finish.

"You choked!" I cried when Neil put me down.

"It's a lot harder than it looks!" Neil huffed, trying to catch his breath. We stared at each other for a second and then burst out laughing.

"Well, ladies and gentlemen!" Donna said, flipping back and forth between pages on her clipboard. "This was a really close one, but it looks like your winners are going to be . . ."

The crowd collectively held its breath, as the Nickelsons stepped forward, their chests thrust out in pride. Neil squeezed my hand.

"The Carlsons!"

A young man and his mom rushed forward from the crowd, jumping up and down excitedly. They had been a last-minute entry to the race, following Donna's explanation that despite the implications of the name, wife-carrying teams did not have to be married to win: "The wife may be your own, or your neighbor's, or you may find one further afield." A mother-son team certainly qualified for the race.

The entry was a smart move. In addition to being the youngest and strongest male in the competition, the kid had motivation. Neil's desire to win the beer paled in comparison to that of a 21-year-old on a college student's budget. I imagine he had quite the party that night.

As it turns out, my prediction was incorrect: Piggybacking on my husband's athleticism is not a surefire win after all. To our great disappointment, we left the Midwest Wife Carrying Championship with neither the beer nor the gold, Estonian-style Barbie and Ken. But I did go home with a prize—my real-life Ken doll.

On paper, Neil and I are very different people, especially when it comes to sport. He's the fast one, and I'm the slow one. He takes race execution seriously, and I goof off and forget to eat. He qualifies for world-class events, and I—well, I sign us up for things like the Midwest Wife Carrying Championship.

But I think that's why we work so well together. For as much as Neil sighs with exasperation when I forget to eat yet again, he's never once said, "I told you so." He just cracks open the can of soda and looks at me with so much affection, I think my heart might burst. And though I will never be as fast as him, I will *woo-hoo* my loudest at everything he does, because I'm his number-one fan and the captain of his cheerleading squad. That's what love is: We carry each other—sometimes literally.

As Neil turned right on Main Street to begin our road trip back to Utah, he reached across the front seat and squeezed my hand.

"So what's next?" he asked. "Synchronized swimming in Bismarck? Tour de Alabama on a tandem bike?"

I laughed. "You can retire now. I promise."

"What?" Neil lifted my hand and brought it to his lips for a kiss. "And miss all the fun?"

17

THE
ULTIMATE HUMAN RACE

SOMEWHERE IN SOUTH AFRICA, I lost my shit.

Neil says he started seeing signs that I was cracking shortly after we landed in Johannesburg. I first noticed I was getting flustered at a campsite outside of Ermelo. But by the time we drove our camper van into the town of Pietermaritzburg, it was clear—I was a ball of raw nerves.

"Are you okay?" Neil asked. When I didn't answer, he reached out and gently touched my arm.

Of course, I'm fucking okay, I wanted to say. This was the third time in as many hours he had asked me that question. But instead, my mouth went dry, and my hands began to shake.

In front of us was a two-story brick home, both levels wrapped in white verandas. Inside, I would pick up a bib number for the oldest and largest ultramarathon in the world—that is, if I could make it inside. It seemed my legs had forgotten how to walk—that, or I was wearing concrete boots. Either way, it was not the most reassuring feeling for someone about to run 56 miles.

"I don't belong here," I said, my lower lip quivering. I would not lose my shit. Not here.

"But you do," Neil replied, putting his hand on my lower back and guiding me toward the two-story brick house. "See? Your name is on that banner." Indeed, it was. And indeed, I lost my shit.

I had been in awe of the Comrades Marathon for years. Several of my friends and colleagues had traveled to South Africa to run it, and every one of them came back with an ethereal glow—it was as if the secret of life had been revealed over the 56 miles of the historic Comrades route between Pietermaritzburg and Durban. The first time the race offered live coverage online, I had clicked on the link out of fleeting curiosity and ended up watching, enraptured, for more than six hours. The stories of the runners in South Africa encompassed everything from tragedy to triumph, and I couldn't look away. Of all the races in the world, the Comrades Marathon topped my bucket list.

Except there was one problem: I didn't belong at a race like Comrades. When I signed up for the race in my 3:00 a.m. registration blitz, I had never run more than 26.2 miles. Completing my first 50-miler on the Pony Express Trail only added a whole new layer of fear—it had taken me more than 13 hours to run 50 miles. How was I supposed to add six more miles to that *and* do it under the 12-hour time limit? My next ultramarathon attempt, Across the Years, had ended with me passed out in a tent, which derailed my confidence even more.

Instead of becoming more comfortable and confident, my progression toward Comrades was marked by a growing, insidious self-doubt. I became obsessed with pace during long runs, checking my watch so often I forgot to look up at other, more important things, like signposts and cracks in the sidewalk. When I came home, Neil would always ask how my run went, and I would always say it was fine. Then I'd go upstairs, lock myself in the bathroom, and hyperventilate in the shower. Things were definitely not fine.

I felt like a fraud and a fool. My pace in training indicated that in order to finish under the 12-hour cutoff, everything would need to go perfectly. I couldn't afford so much as a headwind, and yet I knew that was an impossible ask. If my forays into ultramarathon running had taught me anything, it's that a lot can—and does—go wrong over the course of 50-plus miles.

I confessed this fear to just one person, who quickly tossed aside my concerns. "Oh, come on!" my friend Doug said. "It's on the roads, not the trail. And it's mostly downhill, right? Easy-peasy." His intent was good, but such assurances rang hollow coming from someone who had just won a 100-mile race. Doug had never been in the back of the pack. He didn't know what it felt like to have a cutoff time looming over his head like a guillotine. I did. That I could even admit my firsthand experience with that ominous feeling only served as more evidence that I didn't belong at Comrades.

But I couldn't tell anyone that. I couldn't tell anyone about the race nightmares I had, where my legs would suddenly pixelate and then—*poof!*—disappear, or the one where I would joyfully see the finish line in the distance, only to be hit with a wave of dread as a giant race clock changed from 11 hours and 59 minutes to 12 hours. In that instant, everything in the race went dark, as if someone had flipped a switch that made the entire city of Durban power down. Every time, I'd shoot upright in a cold sweat, frantically fumbling in the dark until I realized it was just a dream.

So I faked it. I did the runs on my training plan every day; then I went home and told Neil everything was fine. I'd then go in the bathroom, look at my average pace for the run, and hyperventilate. Each shallow breath inflated my insecurity like a balloon.

I thought I was doing a good job of faking it. But seeing my name on the banner outside Comrades House in Pietermaritz-burg made it so real. I wanted to go to the race officials and tell them that I had made a huge mistake by signing up; that I was a horrible person for besmirching the race with my presence; that it was disrespectful to the real runners, and I was sorry.

And yet.

And yet! I couldn't walk away. I wanted so badly to be a part of it.

From the moment our plane touched down, I loved everything about South Africa. Neil and I had decided to rent a camper van and road-trip our way from Johannesburg to Cape Town, stopping for Comrades at the halfway point of our trip. Along the way, we braked for elephants and wildebeest, got chased by a wild baboon, got lost (like, dirt-road, tribes-in-robes-and-paint lost), and slept under the brightest stars. *Magical* is the best word I can come up with to describe the country, and even that feels insufficient.

But what I really loved is the enormous pride South Africa has for its runners. When we arrived, the entire country was buzzing with anticipation for "the marathon," as they called it. Every day, the newspapers ran a full-page headline on the race. The event would be broadcast live on every television. Every person we met had a story in connection with the event, whether it was as a participant, a spectator, or a volunteer.

Comrades bills itself as the "Ultimate Human Race," and I was starting to see why: In addition to the 20,000 runners on the course, from all across the globe, an entire country rallied around the event. Their intense, all-consuming love for the

Comrades Marathon and its runners swept me away. Despite my self-doubt, I wanted to at least try to be a part of it.

On race morning, Neil wrapped me in a hug before dropping me at the start line.

"I'll see you in Durban," he said. He would drive the 56 miles to the beach city, where we would camp that night.

Sure, I thought. *If I actually finish.* But I didn't say anything. I couldn't. All I could do was force a tight-lipped smile before giving him a goodbye kiss. I turned around and joined the mass of humanity moving toward the start line. When I looked back, he was gone.

Even before the starting pistol fires, the Comrades Marathon moves as one. Once a runner joins the swarm heading to the start line at Pietermaritzburg City Hall, they yield their independence. The field is one massive living organism; its runners, mere molecules. Even trying to find my starting corral proved futile, as I could only move along with the pressing wave of arms and legs around me and hope I was heading in the right direction.

Then suddenly, everything went still. I panicked. Why was everyone stopping? A man next to me, sensing my alarm, grabbed my hand and patted it calmly. He smiled kindly as he began to sing, joining the 20,000 voices soaring into the purple predawn. This was completely unlike the typical pre-race national anthem routine, with an obligatory hand over the heart while nervously pacing. The song was a traditional folk song, *Shosholoza*, which means "go forward." I watched, mesmerized, at the rapt faces around me. When the song was over, the man squeezed my hand and pointed toward the start line: *Go forward.*

Then a gunshot—*bang!*—and we went forth, spilling into the dark streets of Pietermaritzburg. Five miles passed before I could take a step without brushing elbows or bumping shoulders with another runner. Slowdowns at sharp turns were frequent. At one section, where the route went from a city road to a freeway, a bottleneck formed as runners merged into a single-lane on-ramp. Everyone came to a stop and looked at each other with a shrug and a smile.

As the sun rose and the race progressed through the plains outside of Pietermaritzburg, crowds began to form—gradually at first, then larger and louder as the sun climbed higher in the sky. Every inch of the course, even the most remote spots of the highlands, had people offering relief for runners—be it a row of high fives or a plate of boiled potatoes.

The largest crowds formed at the cutoff points, positioned approximately every 10 miles. At each point was a large gate and a countdown clock to that checkpoint's cutoff time. Arriving at the first one, I saw I had a cushion of 30 minutes.

Shit, I thought. If I slowed down—and with 46 miles to go, this was all but guaranteed—30 minutes wasn't much of a cushion. I balled my fists and took a deep breath. I couldn't worry about that now. I could only try to make it to the next cutoff in time.

Just past the countdown clock, a man stood with a large red sign: REMEMBER YOUR WHY. It seemed like a ridiculous statement. What was the point? The reason I was doing this race was because I was delusional, frankly. I had no business being there. I could only keep running, waiting for the inevitable appearance of a sweep vehicle in my periphery.

The sign appeared again just before the mile 20 cutoff: **REMEMBER YOUR WHY.** I saw it, and then I saw the countdown clock. I hadn't gotten slower. My cushion had actually gotten bigger, with 35 minutes to spare.

Why? I thought. *Because I want to see if I can.*

Just past the halfway point, near the village of Hillcrest, the spectator crowd morphed from adults to children. It turned out, we were running through a massive boarding school campus, which was represented by a large, animated contingency of elementary students. Their exuberant dancing infused my veins with energy and joy. A large banner in a tree denoted that the children were proud students at the school.

Some of the Comrades runners wore multiple bead necklaces, which they handed out to the children as they ran by. The gesture warmed my heart, and I wished I had known to bring some of my own to distribute.

The road through campus curved to the right, where more children awaited. There, another large sign caught my eye: **FULTON SCHOOL FOR THE DEAF ❤S DEAF RUNNERS.**

I came to a dead stop in the road, a hand over my mouth in stunned silence as my eyes welled with tears. I had not expected that. Of course, these students had no way of knowing that I—

or any other runner on the course that day—was deaf. We were from opposite sides of the world, with vastly different stories and vastly different experiences. And yet. And yet!

A passing runner grazed my elbow, shaking me out of my shock. I began running again, slower now, moving to the side of the road so I could be closer to the children. I formed my hand into one of the only signs I knew: *I love you.*

One of the smallest children gasped and pointed first to her ear and then to mine. She flapped a hand at the other children to get their attention and pointed at me. Their eyes widened as they recognized the sign and the hearing aid in my ear. They waved excitedly, their fingers, thumbs, and pinkies extended in response: *I love you, too.*

It was a sign, literally, figuratively. It had to be. I was going to finish this race.

At the next cutoff, mile 30, I had a cushion of 45 minutes. I spied yet another red sign: **REMEMBER YOUR WHY.**

Because I want to see if I can.

I saw the sign again at mile 40, where I dared to alter my answer:

Because I think I can.

As the route descended from the Highlands to the Durban city limits, the crowds became even deeper. Hundreds of thousands of spectators lined the course, chanting, singing, calling out encouragement, offering food or even leg massages if we needed it. I was tired, yet I felt unstoppable.

In the final miles of the race, a large stage had been erected on the side of the road. A band of African drummers pounded out a rhythm so loud, I could feel it vibrate in my rib cage. Without thinking, my footfalls fell in step with the beat. I smiled, looking at the runners ahead of me; they were all doing the same, moving to the beat. The spectators clapped and danced on the side of the road.

Suddenly my arms broke out in goose bumps, and I had to remind myself to breathe. For a surreal, beautiful moment, we were all perfectly in sync. I felt flooded with a euphoria I had never experienced in a race. This was no runner's high—this was a spiritual experience.

Beyond the stage, I could see the striking curved architecture of the Moses Mabhida Stadium, still miles away. I looked at my watch. I would make it and with time to spare. I decided to walk, just for a moment, and take it all in as I passed the final cutoff. Again, the red sign: REMEMBER YOUR WHY.

I laughed out loud, unable to contain my glee. "Because I fucking can!" I whooped. The man holding the sign nodded approvingly and pointed in the direction of the finish line.

The sun was setting when I arrived at the stadium, a beautiful piece of architecture on the beachfront of Durban. In the final stretch to the finish line, runners were routed through a dark tunnel that emerged onto a soccer pitch, surrounded by a roaring stadium and bright lights.

And unlike in my nightmare, this time the lights stayed on.

And instead of fumbling around in the dark in a cold sweat, I got a warm hug from an elderly gentleman as he placed a finisher medal around my neck. I didn't hyperventilate out of fear, but I did find it difficult to breathe as I sobbed into Neil's chest when he hugged me at the finish line—deep, heaving sobs of gratitude and relief and exhaustion.

If this was a dream, I still haven't woken up. And my goose bumps still haven't gone away.

A lot of things could—and should—have gone wrong over the course of 56 miles that day. And yet somehow, everything went exactly right. In all my life, I may never have a race like that again—and if that's the case, that's fine by me. Somewhere along those 56 miles, the secret of life was revealed to me:

I belong.

Epilogue

OPEN SESAME

OVER THE PAST YEAR, I ran hundreds of miles outside of my comfort zone. I took risks, tried new things, pushed myself, and traveled the world, all in the hopes of reengaging with the sport I had once loved and to feel—finally!—what it was to be a real runner. It was only when I lined up for a second time at the start of the Huntsville Marathon—the same race I had grudgingly finished one year prior—that I realized that in all that time, I had never actually figured out the password.

This realization came as no small disappointment. Still, I decided to give the Huntsville Marathon another go. It seemed only fitting as the matching bookend to my year.

After a year away from traditional racing, maybe everything would click into place on my return. Maybe I'd surprise myself with a PR. If the stars aligned, maybe I'd even qualify for Boston, the perfect ending to my fairy tale! I fantasized about how I would finally get to sign off on my story: "Susan Lacke, Real Runner."

But fairy tales are not reality, and running doesn't care about tidy endings. When I arrived at the start line of the marathon, the sky was foggy and smelled of a bonfire. Overnight, a small wildfire three counties over had more than quadrupled in size, fanned by high winds blowing through the area. The Pole Creek Fire was now more than 100,000 acres, covering the state of Utah with nebulous, smoke-filled skies. Wind gusts were still blowing through, but instead of an invigorating breeze of fresh air, we got blasts of dense, smoky, 90-degree haze.

Shortly after the starting gun, I looked down at my watch. At the pace I was going, I would definitely not qualify for Boston. By the time I got to the halfway point, a PR was out of reach, too. I took a puff of my inhaler and stared down the road ahead of me. *All right,* I thought, *let's see what I can salvage from this.*

I decided to start by chasing down the woman 200 yards ahead of me. From there, I'd pick off the next and the next. I always got a boost from passing people. But as I got closer to my first mark, she began to stumble to the left. She shook her head and righted herself, before continuing on for a few more steps. She staggered to the right. She put her arms out to catch her balance, but it proved futile. She went down, hard, on the asphalt.

I sprinted to her collapsed body. She had a hand over her forehead, muttering and moaning.

"Are you okay?" I asked.

She nodded. "I'm good. Just dizzy. Keep going."

"No offense, Andrea," I replied, using the name printed on her bib number. "But you don't look so good."

The runner pulled herself into a sitting position and then pushed herself over to the side of the road. "No, don't stop for me. I'm fine. I just need to sit down for a second."

Another runner came up to us. "Do you need a medic?" she asked. "I'll run ahead and tell them to call for one at the next aid station." She took off over the crest of the hill, and I sat down next to the runner to wait.

"You don't have to stay," she insisted. "I'm fine. I'm actually going to get up in a minute."

"Then I'll get up with you," I said. There was no way I was leaving her. "I could use a break, anyway. Want some water?" I pulled the bite valve off my hydration pack and offered her the tube.

She looked at me gratefully as she took the tube. "I'm Annie," she said.

"Nice to meet you. I'm Susan." I handed her a gel from the stash in my pack.

Annie leaned forward and draped her arms over her knees. She sat in silence for several minutes, sucking on the gel, and then she sighed. "This isn't the way I expected my first marathon to go."

I gave her a pat on the back. "It happens to all of us."

"Yeah?" Annie asked.

"Oh, yeah!" I told her about what had happened to me at Across the Years, where I blacked out while running and came to in my tent with no idea of what had happened or how I'd gotten there.

She laughed. "Okay, that makes me feel a little better."

As we waited for the medic to arrive, Annie asked me if I did a lot of races. "Kind of," I replied. I told her about the year I had just completed, running from the top of the Empire State Building to the bottom of the Grand Canyon.

"That sounds way more fun than this," she sighed, gesturing at the race in front of us. Her disillusionment with running broke my heart. It was her first time attempting a marathon, and she was sure she'd never run again. "Maybe I'm just not a runner," she said, lowering her head in defeat.

"Oh, but you are," I replied firmly. "Trust me."

The authority of that statement took me by surprise: *Trust me.* A year ago, I probably would have sat there in awkward silence. If anything, I would have tried to comfort Annie by saying I wasn't a runner, either. But I didn't feel that way anymore. I felt—dare I say it?—like a runner. A real one.

In the distance, I could see a green all-terrain vehicle heading our way. The medic would be here soon.

"Hey, Annie," I nudged her. "You got family waiting for you?"

"Yeah," she said. "Why?"

"Make them buy you a milkshake and a cheeseburger."

Annie chuckled. "That sounds so good right now."

"And then promise me one thing."

"What's that?"

"You'll try this running thing again."

Annie cracked a wan smile as the medics pulled to the side of the road. I looked down at my watch. If I hurried, I could still make the six-hour cutoff for the marathon.

I did not set a personal best that day. In fact, as finish times go, I set a personal worst. My marathon time was a full hour slower than the year before, and instead of triumphant music at the finish line, I got a worried husband asking, "What took you so long?" It was about as far from a fairy-tale ending as it gets.

But instead of feeling dissatisfied or depressed, I was filled with excitement for Annie's new beginning. I deeply hoped that she would try again. I wanted her to experience firsthand what running is really about—not arbitrary race distances, but adventures. Wild adventures, in the best places with the best people.

"Want to go home?" Neil asked as I exited the finisher's chute. I shook my head as a finish-line volunteer wrapped a space blanket around my shoulders.

"Nah. Let's stay for a bit. I like it here."

We sat on the grass, eating bananas and watching my fellow finishers noshing, rehydrating, laughing, and high-fiving in the feed zone. As far as runners go, everyone here looked as real as it gets. I reflected on the past year. In all the events I had done, had I ever encountered a fake runner? Was there even such a thing? I thought about some of the things that real runners do:

> They partake in the very real act of running, with their very real bodies and very real goals.

> They do it in sprints and ultramarathons and everything in between.

> They do it on tracks and up ski jumps and in pursuit of cheese.

> They do it while wearing split shorts, wacky costumes, or sometimes nothing at all.

> They experience very real pain and very real joy, and they face their very (very) real fears.

> And they do it because they're real runners.

At the beginning of this book, I told you there would be no secret password revealed—that's because there isn't one. Running is a club, all right, but here's the beautiful thing: Anyone is welcome to join.

I never would have started running had it not been for Carlos, who inspired me to start. I never would have kept running had I not been able to ask him the most random and awkward questions about running, such as "Is it normal for my toenail to be black?" or "What the hell is a fartlek?" He was the first real runner I had ever met—and the standard toward which I still strive.

I never would have taken on new challenges had it not been for friends like Heidi, whose one-upmanship tapped into a competitive drive I didn't even know I had, or Dan, who can make any run a party. I never would have found such deep wells of inspiration had I not met the runners of Cuba or South Africa. And though I am technically running toward a finish line, I am really running toward Neil, who always waits for me just beyond. They're all real runners, and I strive every day to be a little more like them.

I had the wrong idea going into this year. I thought "real" running was proven in distance, mile splits, body weight—something that could be quantified. Now I know it can't possibly be contained.

Running is also a very real gift. I'm acutely aware of that—more so now than ever before. There is a very real possibility that one day, my body won't be able to do the boneheaded things I ask of it. I'll have to take the elevator to the top of the Empire State Building or gaze wistfully from the rim of the Grand Canyon. But I will still have my stories. I will forget what my marathon PR was 40 years ago, and that will be fine. Because when I tell my friends' children's children about my adventures in running, no one will ask, "But Aunt Susan, what was your finishing time?" If they do, I will smack them with my cane and reply, "Shut up, child, and listen to this story about Patrick Wilson."

Until then, I will run. I hope you'll join me. All are welcome.

Love,

Susan Lacke

REAL RUNNER

THE ABC'S OF RUNNING

When I first set out to write this book, my editors had originally asked me to put together a how-to for readers, full of tips and training plans and data. They instantly regretted that request, because I am the least-qualified person to write training plans and how-tos and data.

Even after this year, I don't claim to know everything about running—far from it. There are many people far better equipped to prescribe workouts or debate the merits of a forefoot strike versus a heel strike. I don't know how to write a book like that. I do know that running goes beyond the simple act of putting one foot in front of the other. And I know that with every run, I learn a little more. Sometimes the lessons are instantly life changing, while others are small seeds of knowledge that need time to grow into something significant.

I've found that these simple tips and tidbits—a runner's ABC's, if you will—have done more for my running than tweaking my form or doing core work ever could (unless you're my coach, in which case core work is amazing, and I am *totally* typing this while doing a plank).

A **Always remember to pee before heading out on a run.** Even if you don't have to go, talk to your bladder like a kindergartener: "Are you sure? Why don't you just try, okay?"

B **Boobs:** There are many pieces of gear runners can buy on the cheap. A good sports bra is not one of them.

C **Confidence is healthy;** arrogance is not. Don't be that guy.

D **Denial:** Pretending an injury does not exist will not make it go away. Believe me, I've tried.

E **Easy:** Not every run should be a gut-busting speed session. In fact, most of your runs shouldn't be gut-busting speed sessions. Easy runs mean just that—easy. If you can talk (but not sing), you're at the right pace.

F **Failure:** One bad day will teach you more lessons than 20 good ones. Embrace it—you can't learn from your mistakes unless you make them.

G **Google is not a replacement for a real doctor.** A real doctor would never tell you your knee pain may or may not require amputation.

H **Hill repeats:** It's a good thing running uphill sucks so much. It means you have more to look forward to on the way down.

I **Instagram:** Propping a phone up against a rock and running back and forth in front of it 15 times to get a perfect photo does not a #sweatsesh #omghardworkout make.

J **Just do it!** Don't overthink, don't check the weather for the umpteenth time, don't sit on the couch in your run clothes until you feel "ready," and don't whine about how you have to run. Just put on your shoes and go.

K **Kindness:** Help an injured runner. Thank volunteers. Be courteous and encouraging. Say hello. Smile.

L **Logic:** Never sign up for a race [1] when you're injured, [2] within 24 hours of crossing your last finish line, or [3] when you are drunk.

M **Music:** All hail the power of a good playlist during a tough training session. That said, for your safety and the safety of others, rock out with one earbud only.

N **Never:** The faster you remove this word from your vocabulary, the better off you'll be. Allow yourself the possibility of taking on new distances, new trails, new challenges.

O   **Our mothers were right:** Posture matters, especially while running. Stand up straight, child.

P   **Poop:** After your first mid-run "emergency," you'll become more obsessed with this bodily function than ever before, and that's normal. [Pro tip: Coffee usually gets things, er, going before a run.]

Q   **Question quick fixes,** whether a training plan that guarantees speed overnight or a sock that promises to fix your wonky stride. If it sounds too good to be true, it probably is.

R   **Rap music:** "They" say 180 beats per minute is the ideal step count for runners. I had a hard time understanding what that meant until someone told me to run in time with Ludacris's "Move Bitch" and Missy Elliott's "Get Your Freak On."

S   **Six:** There will be days you don't feel like running. Force yourself to do it for only six minutes. If you still don't want to run after that time, turn around and go home. [Spoiler alert: You probably won't go home.]

T   **Tip your massage therapist well,** because you really don't want to piss off the person who puts his elbow in your IT band.

U **Understand your weaknesses and train them.** Sure, the easy stuff is more fun, but the challenging stuff is what makes you better.

V **Voices:** Now and then, self-doubt will creep in: I'll never be fast/go far/finish first. The voices in your head are liars. You're doing great. Keep going.

W **Weight:** Training for a marathon is not a guaranteed way to lose weight. Yes, you burn a lot of calories, but you're also hungry all the damn time. You try to turn down a second (third, ninth) slice of pizza after a 20-miler and tell me how that goes.

X **eXplore:** Don't run a rut in the same path every day like a trained circus pony. Get out and get lost. Many good stories begin where the sidewalk ends.

Y **You:** Running is about you and what you want to accomplish—not your friend who wants you to run an ultramarathon, not your spouse who thinks you should wear different shoes, not the internet forums that argue over the best crosstraining, not some asshat running-book author (ahem). Consult these people for advice if you wish, but in the end, choose the goals and methods that work for you.

Z   **Zippers:** Don't run in a single item of clothing where zippers come in contact with skin, or you'll find yourself chafed beyond comprehension. This may be the most important (and most painful) running lesson I've learned.

AUTHOR'S NOTE

The stories in this book are true. The order of some events may have been rejiggered for flow, and some names have been changed to protect the innocent (and in some cases, the guilty). But honestly, you can't make this stuff up.

It's important to note that the stories are told from my perspective. I may have missed something on the periphery—I am deaf, after all, so I "hear" what I see in front of me. Whenever possible, I asked participants at each event to confirm the accuracy of my account and fill in anything that I may have missed while looking in another direction. As my friend Heidi said, "You don't miss anything when you look away. Mostly we just talk shit behind your back." (To be fair, they also talk shit to my face.)

Though I strongly encourage you to experience one or more of these events yourself, the legal folks at my publisher would like me to make it clear that any WTF-ery you choose to engage in is of your own doing. We are not responsible for death, dismemberment, and/or incriminating photos that may result from stunts inspired by this book.

(But seriously—go out there and get your weird on. It's way fun. If you need a partner in asshattery, tweet me @SusanLacke.)

ACKNOWLEDGMENTS

I do not take for granted that I have the best job in the world. I credit this to the questionable decision-making skills of Renee Jardine and the VeloPress team, who let me tag along like an annoying little sister.

Casey Blaine's exceptional work has ruined me for all other editors. She doesn't know this, but before we signed the contract for this book, I added a few lines, and now we are legally married. You can't quit me, editorwife.

This is the second book of mine Sarah Gorecki has proofread or production edited, so if you see her, please give her a fist bump and/or a shot of tequila. God knows she's earned it.

Dave Trendler and Kara Mannix do not flinch at my absurd marketing ideas. They just sigh, say, "For the last time, Lacke, NO MONKEYS," and then come up with a bona fide plan that actually works.

There were a lot of moving parts to address in the research and execution of this book. Many thanks to the race directors, historians, volunteers, participants, and spectators who gave me information, inspiration, and one hell of a good time.

I would not have made it through the year in one piece without Heidi Lueb's coaching and Dr. Nate Bernatz's mad dry-needling skills. In their own ways, they each were a massive pain in my ass. All those f-bombs really meant "Thank you," I swear.

Meghan Boyle, Kristen "Seabiscuit" Seymour, and Matthew LaPlante helped me move from sitting in my underwear, freaking out about writing this book, to sitting in my underwear, actually writing this book. Thanks for talking me out of my panic spiral.

Being married to Neil Manville is the greatest adventure ever. Of all the stories I get to tell, ours is my favorite.

ABOUT THE AUTHOR

Susan Lacke is a writer, professor, and endurance athlete whose work regularly appears in *Competitor, Triathlete, Women's Running,* and *Salt Lake* magazines. She lives in Arizona with three animals: a cattle dog, a miniature pinscher, and a freakishly tall husband named Neil. Lacke claims to be of sound mind, though this has yet to be substantiated by a medical professional. She is the author of *Life's Too Short to Go So F*cking Slow.*

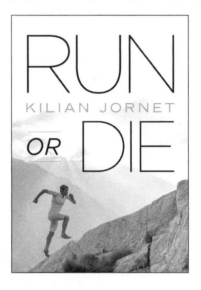